David

THE NAKED ASTRONAUT

THE NAKED ASTRONAUT

Poems on Birth and Birthdays

AN ANTHOLOGY EDITED BY

René Graziani

faber and faber

LONDON · BOSTON

First published in 1983
by Faber and Faber Limited
3 Queen Square London WC1N 3AU
Phototypeset by Wyvern Typesetting Limited, Bristol
Printed in Great Britain by
Redwood Burn Ltd, Trowbridge, Wiltshire
All rights reserved

Selection and Preface © René Graziani, 1983

British Library Cataloguing in Publication Data

The naked astronaut: poems on birth and birthdays.
1. Childbirth poetry
2. English poetry
I. Graziani, René
PR1195.C/   PR1195.B/

ISBN 0–571–13119–0
ISBN 0–571–13193–X Pbk

Library of Congress Data has been applied for.

For Dorothy, George, Edmund and Millie

CONTENTS

15

PREFACE

Birth and birthdays are times for celebration—a fact overwhelmingly reflected in this anthology. Angels, good fairies, godparents, prayers, good wishes and the rite of poetry itself spring up protectively around the birth event. Rejoicing is not the only note, however. The variety of poets' reactions can be assessed only by reading the poems themselves. Yet for mixed feelings about birthdays we might consider Swift. On his own birthday, he liked to recite Job's curses on his birth, whereas in a poem to Stella on hers, he gives thanks for her friendship and virtues. Rarely does a poet greet his own birthday with unironic joy, though Dylan Thomas celebrates his thirtieth unequivocally. Birthdays, it seems, lend themselves naturally to irony. And as for the birth image itself, irony approaches its extreme limit in Thomas Merton's prose-poem on the bombing of Hiroshima.

Positive aversion to birthdays does exist. Descartes, for instance, kept his birthday a secret to protect himself from horoscope makers—understandably enough, since several of his friends went into a decline and one actually died (Descartes believed) because a horoscope had predicted ill-health. Fears about birth were widespread: Anne Bradstreet touchingly records her concern for husband and children should she not survive labour, and infant mortality informs Lord Herbert of Cherbury's tougher lines on the birth of Lady Pembroke's child: "And tis no matter how it shews/All I care is if the child grows." (Lady Pembroke had lost two children already.) Welcoming birth sometimes coincides with death, as in Joyce's "Ecce Puer" and Jack Clemo's "Charlotte Nichols". Still, for reasons of category, I decided to stop there and not to include some deeply moving poems on miscarriages, stillbirths and infant deaths, though I have included other sorts of casualty.

There were few obscurities to unravel, largely because birth and birthdays on the whole are treated familiarly and directly: hence editorial interpolations are few. I have divided up the poems by their occasions and have disregarded chronology. But since some sense of history emerged in the collecting process, a few points are offered here.

Only quite recently have poets, especially women, taken possession of the whole physical and psychological experience of birth. The Greek poets responded to birth almost exclusively through cosmogonies and the legends of gods, especially fantastic births from heads, thighs, foam, eggs. Milton's birth of Sin and Death and Gargantua's emergence from his mother's ear belong to this tradition. Apart from some slight verses accompanying presents, human births or birth-days are virtually absent from what survives of Greek poetry. The one late literary development was the birthday speech.

Birth poems exist in some oral cultures. An elaborate example (too anthropologically arcane for inclusion here) is the *Song of Muu*, a Cuna Indian medicine man's incantation for a difficult birth. But birthday poetry as we know it is Roman in origin and appears to have been rooted in the religious observances dedicated to the Genius or Juno, a personal divinity who oversaw the individual's fortunes. Horace, Ovid, Martial, Propertius, Tibullus and Sulpicia all compose festal birthday poems for patrons, friends, mistresses, wives or themselves. With the exception of seminal passages in Lucretius (and Alcmena's travail in the *Metamorphoses*), Roman poetry about birth itself really amounts to one great poem, Virgil's Fourth Eclogue (c. 40 BC), which early Christians read as Messianic. A domestic pastoral scene of eagerly anticipated birth is the stage for a grand prophecy of the restoration of the Golden Age. Virgil's conception of a peace-bringing child looks rather like an "answer" to Catullus's poem on the wedding of Peleus and Thetis—when the Fates proclaim the fortunes of their fearless warrior son Achilles, destined to choke a river with corpses. Later Roman wedding poems do not notably feature birth, however.

With Christianity and the mystery of the Incarnation, birth acquired a new centrality. Nativity hymns sprang naturally from the liturgy: Luke's *Magnificat* supplied a precedent for Christian Latin poets to follow in celebrating the whole story of Christ's birth. Later this celebration reached the vernacular in the widespread form of the carol, a song that originally accompanied round dances. Yet the Nativity carol seeded no poetry for other births, it would seem—though it was fertile in lullabies. Much as the New Year, Christmas became a sort of universal birthday, when the blessedness of all human birth was comprehended in the humble arrival of the God Child. And the tragic shadow cast by the Passion on the joyous event of Christ's birth ensured that the opposites of pain and joy latent in the birth image were finally drawn into full literary consciousness. The rest of the Christian calendar, however, offered few openings for any further secular branching out: with the exception of Mary and John the Baptist, the Church celebrated no natal feasts, observing instead the Saints' death days as the real birth into eternal life. Donne's long poem on such a birth–death, *The Anniversaries*, is not represented in this collection though, because excerpts convey only a feeble idea of its cumulative majesty.

Elizabethan and Jacobean birth poetry is predominantly fictive—ranging from the mythic variety of Spenser in *The Faerie Queene* to the tragic realism of the Duchess of Malfi's childbirth in Webster's play. Poetry addressing live occasions got off to a slow start in the Renaissance. Latin *natalitia* remained rarities. Queen Elizabeth's public celebrations took place on her name day, on her coronation anniversary and on New Year's Day. Her actual birthday, 7 September, generated only a few slight poems (complimenting the month for bearing her) until Shakespeare produced a Virgilian prophecy for her christening in *Henry VIII*. Philip Sidney's birth was marked by the planting of an oak, and some birthdays were celebrated with feasting—the repast that Orlando interrupts in the forest of Arden was a birthday feast in Lodge's original story—but poetry played no part until Ben Jonson, taking his cue from Horace, thought of adding a poet's voice to the birthday celebrations for Sir Henry Sidney. (There is no evidence I know of to support recent speculation that Shakespeare's Sonnets first saw the light as birthday presentations to William Herbert.) Jonson, like Milton after him, became an enthusiastic occasional poet and continued with birth and birthday poems to other patrons, including Charles I and the whole royal family—creating in the process the role of Poet Laureate. While Jonson sometimes held a mirror of virtue up to his recipients, the approach was essentially festive, but rococo compliment soon overtook most laureate productions, and the worst birthday odes of 1690 to 1820 may be judged from the squibs that I include: the best can be sampled in Nick Russell's *Poets by Appointment* (Poole, Blandford Press/New York, Sterling, 1981). For some Hanoverians, of course, the music must have been the main attraction. Music still helps—as we see in Britten's delightful A *Birthday Handsel* (1978) which set to music poems by Robert Burns. And surely Sir John Betjeman's forthright greeting to the Queen Mother is crying out for a tune?

The extension of greetings to ordinary friends, as distinct from patrons, seems to have been slow: I cannot put a date to it, though, predictably, it flourished in the Augustan period. For Swift, the easy social voice for this basic rite of friendship lay to hand in the shared style of the period, and he lets it find deeper tones as he treats goodness and ageing with witty seriousness. (Ageing, surprisingly, had not been a Roman theme on the occasion.) New accents appear with Blake and Wordsworth: joy and wonder at birth, but also a more passionate feeling of "every infant's cry of fear" and of "shades of the prison house" closing in on the grown man. During the nineteenth century popular culture takes possession of both birth and birthdays with effusions of sentiment and humour. Aestheticism accepts and transforms the sentiment. Three great modern poets, Yeats, Auden and Dylan Thomas, both make the occasions poetically their own and inspire others. Yeats, indeed, whose tall figure dominated many varied scenes, also brings home how confined a stage the birthday is—yet few poets have left a deeper impression than Yeats when marking his fiftieth. In the last forty years women's birth experiences have been fashioned into poetry by Sylvia Plath and others.

To the best of my knowledge, the subject of birth and birthdays has not been anthologized before, although a collection for children entitled *Birthday Candles Burning Bright*, compiled by S. and J. E. Brewton, was published in 1960. Constraints of space have forced me to omit many poems that I would have liked to include, but I hope this selection will appeal to all those who, like the poets represented here, regard birth itself and every succeeding anniversary as an occasion for reflection.

RENÉ GRAZIANI
April 1983

Birth and Good Wishes

"THE ANGEL THAT PRESIDED O'ER MY BIRTH"

The Angel that presided o'er my birth
Said, "Little creature, form'd of Joy & Mirth,
"Go love without the help of any Thing on Earth."

WILLIAM BLAKE

"THE CHILD IS LIKE A SAILOR CAST UP BY THE SEA"

The child is like a sailor cast up by the sea,
Lying naked on the shore, unable to speak,
Helpless, when first it comes to the light of day,
Shed from the womb through all the pains of labour,
And fills the place with cries as well it might,
Having a life of so many ills before it.
Yet flocks and herds, to say nothing of wild beasts,
Don't need a rattle or anything of that kind
Nor even a nurse to feed them with baby-talk:
Nor do they need sets of clothes for summer and winter.
One may add that they don't need weapons or high walls
To keep them safe, they find themselves perfectly happy
Walking around in a world which produces plenty.

LUCRETIUS

From *De Rerum Natura*, Book 5 (trans. C. H. Sisson)

BORN YESTERDAY
for Sally Amis

Tightly-folded bud,
I have wished you something
None of the others would:
Not the usual stuff
About being beautiful,
Or running off a spring
Of innocence and love—
They will all wish you that,
And should it prove possible,
Well, you're a lucky girl.

But if it shouldn't, then
May you be ordinary;
Have, like other women,
An average of talents:
Not ugly, not good-looking,
Nothing uncustomary
To pull you off your balance,
That, unworkable itself,
Stops all the rest from working.
In fact, may you be dull—
If that is what a skilled,
Vigilant, flexible,
Unemphasized, enthralled
Catching of happiness is called.

PHILIP LARKIN

THE NATIVITY CHANT
BY MEG MERRILIES

Canny moment, lucky fit;
Is the lady lighter yet?
Be it lad, or be it lass,
Sign wi' cross, and sain wi' mass.

Trefoil, vervain, John's-wort, dill,
Hinders witches of their will;
Weel is them, that weel may
Fast upon Saint Andrew's day.

Saint Bride and her brat,
Saint Colme and her cat,
Saint Michael and his spear,
Keep the house frae reif and wear.

SIR WALTER SCOTT
From *Guy Mannering*

TO MAYSTRES ISABELL PENNELL

By Saynt Mary, my lady,
Your mammy and your dady
Brought forth a godely babi!
   My mayden Isabell,
Reflaring rosabell,
The flagrant camamell;
   The ruddy rosary,
The soverayne rosemary,
The praty strawbery;
   The columbyne, the nepte,
The jeloffer well set,
The propre vyolet;
   Enuwyd, your colowre
Is lyke the dasy flowre
After the Aprill showre;
   Sterre of the morow gray,
The blossom on the spray,
The fresshest flowre of May!
   Maydenly demure,
Of womanhode the lure;
Wherfore, I make you sure,
   It were an hevenly helth,
It were an endeles welth,
A lyfe for God hymselfe,
   To here this nightingale
Amonge the byrdes smale,
Warbelynge in the vale:
   Dug, dug, jug, jug,
Good yere and good luk,
With chuk, chuk, chuk, chuk.

JOHN SKELTON

MUNDUS ET INFANS

for Arthur and Angelyn Stevens

Kicking his mother until she let go of his soul
Has given him a healthy appetite: clearly, her rôle
    In the New Order must be
To supply and deliver his raw materials free;
    Should there be any shortage,
She will be held responsible; she also promises
To show him all such attentions as befit his age.
    Having dictated peace,

With one fist clenched behind his head, heel drawn up
        to thigh
The cocky little ogre dozes off, ready,
    Though, to take on the rest
Of the world at the drop of a hat or the mildest
    Nudge of the impossible,
Resolved, cost what it may, to seize supreme power and
Sworn to resist tyranny to the death with all
    Forces at his command.

A pantheist not a solipsist, he co-operates
With a universe of large and noisy feeling-states
    Without troubling to place
Them anywhere special, for, to his eyes, Funnyface
    Or Elephant as yet
Mean nothing. His distinction between Me and Us
Is a matter of taste; his seasons are Dry and Wet;
    He thinks as his mouth does.

Still his loud iniquity is still what only the
Greatest of saints become—someone who does not lie:
    He because he cannot
Stop the vivid present to think, they by having got
    Past reflection into
A passionate obedience in time. We have our Boy-
Meets-Girl era of mirrors and muddle to work through,
    Without rest, without joy.

Therefore we love him because his judgements are so
Frankly subjective that his abuse carries no
    Personal sting. We should
Never dare offer our helplessness as a good
    Bargain, without at least
Promising to overcome a misfortune we blame
History or Banks or the Weather for: but this beast
    Dares to exist without shame.

Let him praise our Creator with the top of his voice,
Then, and the motions of his bowels; let us rejoice
    That he lets us hope, for
He may never become a fashionable or
    Important personage:
However bad he may be, he has not yet gone mad;
Whoever we are now, we were no worse at his age;
    So of course we ought to be glad

When he bawls the house down. Has he not a perfect
        right
To remind us at every moment how we quite
    Rightly expect each other
To go upstairs or for a walk if we must cry over
    Spilt milk, such as our wish
That, since, apparently, we shall never be above
Either or both, we had never learned to distinguish
    Between hunger and love?

                                        W. H. AUDEN

ON THE BIRTH OF A POSTHUMOUS
CHILD, BORN IN PECULIAR
CIRCUMSTANCES OF
FAMILY DISTRESS

Sweet floweret, pledge o' meikle love,
　　And ward o' mony a prayer,
What heart o' stane wad thou na move,
　　Sae helpless, sweet, and fair.

November hirples o'er the lea,
　　Chill, on thy lovely form;
And gane, alas! the sheltering tree,
　　Should shield thee frae the storm.

May HE who gives the rain to pour,
　　And wings the blast to blaw,
Protect thee frae the driving shower,
　　The bitter frost and snaw.

May HE, the friend of woe and want,
　　Who heals life's various stounds,
Protect and guard the mother plant,
　　And heal her cruel wounds.

But late she flourished, rooted fast,
　　Fair on the summer morn:
Now, feebly bends she, in the blast,
　　Unsheltered and forlorn.

Blest be thy bloom, thou lovely gem,
　　Unscathed by ruffian hand!
And from thee many a parent stem
　　Arise to deck our land.

                                    ROBERT BURNS

SERENADE FOR STRINGS

for Peter

I

At nine from behind the door
The tap tapping
Is furtive, insistent:
Recurrent, imperative
The I AM crying
Exhorting, compelling.

At eleven louder!
Wilderness shaking
Boulders uprolling
Mountains creating

And deep in the cavern
No longer the hammer
Faintly insistent
No longer the pickaxe
Desperate to save us
But minute by minute
The terrible knocking
God at the threshold!
Knocking down darkness
Battering daylight.

II

O green field
O sun soaked
On lavish emerald
Blade and sharp bud piercing
O green field
Cover and possess me
Shield me in brightness now
From the knocking
The terrible knocking. . . .

III

Again . . . Again . . . O again,
Midnight. A new day.
Day of days
Night of nights
Lord of lords.

Good Lord deliver us
Deliver us of the new lord
Too proud for prison
Too urgent for the grave . . .
Deliver us, deliver us.

O God the knocking
The knocking attacking
No breath to fight it
No thought to bridge it
Bare body wracked and writhing
Hammered and hollowed
To airless heaving.

IV

The clock now. Morning.
Morning come creeping
Scrublady slishing
And sloshing the waxway
And crying O world
Come clean
Clean for the newborn
The sun soon rising . . .

Rising and soaring
On into high gear . . .
Sudden knowledge!
Easy speedway
Open country
Hills low-flying
Birds up-brooding
Clouds caressing
A burning noon-day . . .

Now double wing-beat
Breasting body
Till cloudways open
Heaven trembles:
   And blinding
      searing
         terrifying
            cry!

The final bolt has fallen,
The firmament is riven.

V

Now it is done.
Relax. Release.
And here, behold your handiwork:
Behold—a man!
DOROTHY LIVESAY

MORNING SONG

Love set you going like a fat gold watch.
The midwife slapped your footsoles, and your bald cry
Took its place among the elements.

Our voices echo, magnifying your arrival. New statue.
In a drafty museum, your nakedness
Shadows our safety. We stand round blankly as walls.

I'm no more your mother
Than the cloud that distils a mirror to reflect its own slow
Effacement at the wind's hand.

All night your moth-breath
Flickers among the flat pink roses. I wake to listen:
A far sea moves in my ear.

One cry, and I stumble from bed, cow-heavy and floral
In my Victorian nightgown.
Your mouth opens clean as a cat's. The window square

Whitens and swallows its dull stars. And now you try
Your handful of notes;
The clear vowels rise like balloons.

SYLVIA PLATH

CHILDBIRTH

When, on the bearing mother, death's
Door opened its furious inch,
Instant of struggling and blood,
The commonplace became so strange

There was not looking at table or chair:
Miracle struck out the brain
Of order and ordinary: bare
Onto the heart the earth dropped then

With whirling quarters, the axle cracked,
Through that miracle-breached bed
All the dead could have got back;
With shriek and heave and spout of blood

The huge-eyed looming horde from
Under the floor of the heart, that run
To the madman's eye-corner came
Deafening towards light, whereon

A child whimpered upon the bed,
Frowning ten-toed ten-fingered birth
Put the skull back about the head
Righted the stagger of the earth.

TED HUGHES

"THOUGH BODIES ARE APART"

Though bodies are apart
The dark hours so confine
And fuse our hearts, sure, death
Will find no way between.

Narrow this hour, that bed;
But room for us to explore
Pain's long-drawn equator,
The farthest ice of fear.

Storm passes east, recurs:
The beakèd lightnings stoop:
The sky falls down: the clouds
Are wrung to the last drop.

Another day is born now.
Woman, your work is done.
This is the end of labour.
Come out into the sun!

C. DAY LEWIS
From *From Feathers to Iron*

ANIMULA

"Issues from the hand of God, the simple soul"
To a flat world of changing lights and noise,
To light, dark, dry or damp, chilly or warm;
Moving between the legs of tables and of chairs,
Rising or falling, grasping at kisses and toys,
Advancing boldly, sudden to take alarm,
Retreating to the corner of arm and knee,
Eager to be reassured, taking pleasure
In the fragrant brilliance of the Christmas tree,
Pleasure in the wind, the sunlight and the sea;
Studies the sunlit pattern on the floor
And running stags around a silver tray;
Confounds the actual and the fanciful,
Content with playing-cards and kings and queens,
What the fairies do and what the servants say.
The heavy burden of the growing soul
Perplexes and offends more, day by day;
Week by week, offends and perplexes more
With the imperatives of "is" and "seems"
And may and may not, desire and control.
The pain of living and the drug of dreams
Curl up the small soul in the window seat
Behind the *Encyclopaedia Britannica*.
Issues from the hand of time the simple soul
Irresolute and selfish, misshapen, lame,
Unable to fare forward or retreat,
Fearing the warm reality, the offered good,
Denying the importunity of the blood,
Shadow of its own shadows, spectre in its own gloom,
Leaving disordered papers in a dusty room;
Living first in the silence after the viaticum.

Pray for Guiterriez, avid of speed and power,
For Boudin, blown to pieces,
For this one who made a great fortune,
And that one who went his own way.
Pray for Floret, by the boarhound slain between the yew
    trees,
Pray for us now and at the hour of our birth.

T. S. ELIOT

FROST AT MIDNIGHT

The Frost performs its secret ministry,
Unhelped by any wind. The owlet's cry
Came loud—and hark, again! loud as before.
The inmates of my cottage, all at rest,
Have left me to that solitude, which suits
Abstruser musings: save that at my side
My cradled infant slumbers peacefully.
'Tis calm indeed! so calm, that it disturbs
And vexes meditation with its strange
And extreme silentness. Sea, hill, and wood,
This populous village! Sea, and hill, and wood,
With all the numberless goings-on of life,
Inaudible as dreams! the thin blue flame
Lies on my low-burnt fire, and quivers not;
Only that film, which fluttered on the grate,
Still flutters there, the sole unquiet thing.
Methinks, its motion in this hush of nature
Gives it dim sympathies with me who live,
Making it a companionable form,
Whose puny flaps and freaks the idling Spirit

By its own moods interprets, every where
Echo or mirror seeking of itself,
And makes a toy of Thought.

                                      But O! how oft,
How oft, at school, with most believing mind,
Presageful, have I gazed upon the bars,
To watch that fluttering *stranger*! and as oft
With unclosed lids, already had I dreamt
Of my sweet birth-place, and the old church-tower,
Whose bells, the poor man's only music, rang
From morn to evening, all the hot Fair-day,
So sweetly, that they stirred and haunted me
With a wild pleasure, falling on mine ear
Most like articulate sounds of things to come!
So gazed I, till the soothing things, I dreamt,
Lulled me to sleep, and sleep prolonged my dreams!
And so I brooded all the following morn,
Awed by the stern preceptor's face, mine eye
Fixed with mock study on my swimming book:
Save if the door half opened, and I snatched
A hasty glance, and still my heart leaped up,
For still I hoped to see the *stranger's* face,
Townsman, or aunt, or sister more beloved,
My play-mate when we both were clothed alike!

Dear Babe, that sleepest cradled by my side,
Whose gentle breathings, heard in this deep calm,
Fill up the interspersèd vacancies
And momentary pauses of the thought!
My babe so beautiful! it thrills my heart
With tender gladness, thus to look at thee,
And think that thou shalt learn far other lore,
And in far other scenes! For I was reared
In the great city, pent 'mid cloisters dim,
And saw nought lovely but the sky and stars.
But *thou*, my babe! shalt wander like a breeze
By lakes and sandy shores, beneath the crags
Of ancient mountain, and beneath the clouds,
Which image in their bulk both lakes and shores
And mountain crags: so shalt thou see and hear
The lovely shapes and sounds intelligible
Of that eternal language, which thy God
Utters, who from eternity doth teach
Himself in all, and all things in himself.
Great universal Teacher! he shall mould
Thy spirit, and by giving make it ask.

Therefore all seasons shall be sweet to thee,
Whether the summer clothe the general earth
With greenness, or the redbreast sit and sing
Betwixt the tufts of snow on the bare branch
Of mossy apple-tree, while the nigh thatch
Smokes in the sun-thaw; whether the eave-drops fall
Heard only in the trances of the blast,
Or if the secret ministry of frost
Shall hang them up in silent icicles,
Quietly shining to the quiet Moon.

SAMUEL TAYLOR COLERIDGE

TO AN INFANT DAUGHTER

Sweet gem of infant fairy-flowers!
Thy smiles on life's unclosing hours,
Like sunbeams lost in summer showers.
    They wake my fears;
When reason knows its sweets and sours,
    They'll change to tears.

God help thee, little senseless thing!
Thou, daisy-like of early spring
Of ambush'd winter's hornet sting
    Hast yet to tell;
Thou know'st not what tomorrows bring:
    I wish thee well.

But thou art come, and soon or late
'Tis thine to meet the frowns of fate,
The harpy grin of envy's hate,
    And mermaid-smiles
Of worldly folly's luring bait,
    That youth beguiles.

And much I wish, whate'er may be
The lot, my child, that falls to thee,
Nature may never let thee see
    Her glass betimes
But keep thee from my failings free—
    Nor itch at rhymes.

Lord help thee in thy coming years
If thy mad father's picture 'pears
Predominant!—his feeling fears
    And jingling starts;
I'd freely now gi' vent to tears
    To ease my heart.

May thou, unknown to rhyming bother,
Be ignorant as is thy mother,
And in thy manners such another,
    Save sin's nigh quest;
And then with 'scaping this and t'other
    Thou mayst be blest.

Lord knows my heart, it loves thee much:
And may my feelings, aches, and such,
The pains I meet in folly's clutch
    Be never thine:
Child, it's a tender string to touch,
    That sounds "Thou'rt mine".

JOHN CLARE

A PRAYER FOR MY DAUGHTER

Once more the storm is howling, and half hid
Under this cradle-hood and coverlid
My child sleeps on. There is no obstacle
But Gregory's wood and one bare hill
Whereby the haystack- and roof-levelling wind,
Bred on the Atlantic, can be stayed:
And for an hour I have walked and prayed
Because of the great gloom that is in my mind.

I have walked and prayed for this young child an hour
And heard the sea-wind scream upon the tower,
And under the arches of the bridge, and scream
In the elms above the flooded stream;
Imagining in excited reverie
That the future years had come,
Dancing to a frenzied drum,
Out of the murderous innocence of the sea.

May she be granted beauty and yet not
Beauty to make a stranger's eye distraught,
Or hers before a looking-glass, for such,
Being made beautiful overmuch,
Consider beauty a sufficient end,
Lose natural kindness and maybe
The heart-revealing intimacy
That chooses right, and never find a friend.

Helen being chosen found life flat and dull
And later had much trouble from a fool,
While that great Queen, that rose out of the spray,
Being fatherless could have her way
Yet chose a bandy-legged smith for man.
It's certain that fine women eat
A crazy salad with their meat
Whereby the Horn of Plenty is undone.

In courtesy I'd have her chiefly learned;
Hearts are not had as a gift but hearts are earned
By those that are not entirely beautiful;
Yet many, that have played the fool
For beauty's very self, has charm made wise,
And many a poor man that has roved,
Loved and thought himself beloved,
From a glad kindness cannot take his eyes.

May she become a flourishing hidden tree
That all her thoughts may like the linnet be,
And have no business but dispensing round
Their magnanimities of sound,
Nor but in merriment begin a chase,
Nor but in merriment a quarrel.
O may she live like some green laurel
Rooted in one dear perpetual place.

My mind, because the minds that I have loved,
The sort of beauty that I have approved,
Prosper but little, has dried up of late,
Yet knows that to be choked with hate
May well be of all evil chances chief.
If there's no hatred in a mind
Assault and battery of the wind
Can never tear the linnet from the leaf.

An intellectual hatred is the worst,
So let her think opinions are accursed.
Have I not seen the loveliest woman born
Out of the mouth of Plenty's horn,
Because of her opinionated mind
Barter that horn and every good
By quiet natures understood
For an old bellows full of angry wind?

Considering that, all hatred driven hence,
The soul recovers radical innocence
And learns at last that it is self-delighting,
Self-appeasing, self-affrighting,
And that its own sweet will is Heaven's will;
She can, though every face should scowl
And every windy quarter howl
Or every bellows burst, be happy still.

And may her bridegroom bring her to a house
Where all's accustomed, ceremonious;
For arrogance and hatred are the wares
Peddled in the thoroughfares.
How but in custom and in ceremony
Are innocence and beauty born?
Ceremony's a name for the rich horn,
And custom for the spreading laurel tree.

W. B. YEATS

A PRAYER FOR MY SON

Bid a strong ghost stand at the head
That my Michael may sleep sound,
Nor cry, nor turn in the bed
Till his morning meal come round;
And may departing twilight keep
All dread afar till morning's back,
That his mother may not lack
Her fill of sleep.

Bid the ghost have sword in fist:
Some there are, for I avow
Such devilish things exist,
Who have planned his murder, for they know
Of some most haughty deed or thought
That waits upon his future days,
And would through hatred of the bays
Bring that to nought.

Though You can fashion everything
From nothing every day, and teach
The morning stars to sing,
You have lacked articulate speech
To tell Your simplest want, and known,
Wailing upon a woman's knee,
All of that worst ignominy
Of flesh and bone;

And when through all the town there ran
The servants of Your enemy,
A woman and a man,
Unless the Holy Writings lie,
Hurried through the smooth and rough
And through the fertile and waste,
Protecting, till the danger past,
With human love.

W. B. YEATS

"THE WINTERS CLOSE, SPRINGS OPEN, NO CHILD STIRS"

XVII

The winters close, Springs open, no child stirs
under my withering heart, O seasoned heart
God grudged his aid.
All things else soil like a shirt.
Simon is much away. My executive stales.
The town came through for the cartway by the pales,
but my patience is short,
I revolt from, I am like, these savage foresters

XVIII

whose passionless dicker in the shade, whose glance
impassive & scant, belie their murderous cries
when quarry seems to show.
Again I must have been wrong, twice.
Unwell in a new way. Can that begin?
God brandishes. O love, O I love. Kin,
gather. My world is strange
and merciful, ingrown months, blessing a swelling
        trance.

XIX

So squeezed, wince you I scream? I love you & hate
off with you. Ages! *Useless.* Below my waist
he has me in Hell's vise.
Stalling. He let go. Come back: brace
me somewhere. No. No. Yes! everything down
hardens I press with horrible joy down
my back cracks like a wrist
shame I am voiding oh behind it is too late

XX

hide me forever I work thrust I must free
now I all muscles & bones concentrate
what is living from dying?
Simon I must leave you so untidy
Monster you are killing me Be sure
I'll have you later Women do endure
I can *can* no longer
and it passes the wretched trap whelming and I am me

drencht & powerful, I did it with my body!
One proud tug greens Heaven. Marvellous,
unforbidding Majesty.
Swell, imperious bells. I fly.
Mountainous, woman not breaks and will bend:
sways God nearby: anguish comes to an end.
Blossomed Sarah, and I
blossom. Is that thing alive? I hear a famisht howl.

JOHN BERRYMAN
From "Homage to Mistress Bradstreet"

YEARS LATER

They tied my mother's legs when I was born.

You ask my sister: she must know it all,
She must remember.
                    Eighteen years ago
They tied my mother's legs with her own shawl.

I felt their laughter shaking in her blood.
That was my world before I felt the world,
Their booted laughter washed through waves of blood.

They laughed, and tied her legs: they always did.

I felt her shuddering as I beat my head
Against the bone, withdrew, then beat again,
Again, and then again: my splintering skull
Trying to find the mouth that led to air
And to the sounds of laughter:

                            tight as teeth
The lips were pressed, and still I beat, and still,
Feeling her screams like splashes in the tide
That took me in its rhythms up to where
The world began, and tight lips turned me back.
There was no world: only those twisting tides,
The choking blood, my torn and twisted head,
The dying sound of laughter in the dark.

LAURENCE LERNER

"THE CELL LAY INSIDE HER BODY"

The cell lay inside her body
(calm as my arm now lies
between her legs).
The cell grew. It divided.
Went on dividing—clunk!
Twist and twist again the helix flipped
and—clunk!
And twist again—clunk! Bravo!
Until it was all happening on all sides
at all times
(like a plant growing at night)
like a great factory
pounding and hissing and turning corners,
pushing out new seaweed shapes
like hands and ears and feet
turning human . . .

Yet she slept. Yet she walked,
through the day. Like a slow plant.
Pretending it wasn't happening,
this cracking of mountains,
this breaking of stone,
this multiplication of the five loaves
and still there was more
and still there was more—
five thousand thousand million cells.

And now, here he is!
He weeps, he cries, he laughs,
he gives all manner of signs of life—
what a colourful wind-kicking rag he is!

A kite who lunges at the sky.
And his dark plant-time
is slipping out of sight
through the closing fontanelle.

I stand to him as the slow plants stand to me—
tender and attender, watcher and blesser.
We breathe exchanges.
I give him my face. He gives me his smile.
I give him my hand. He bites it.

MURRAY EDMOND
From "A Patching Together", 3

"ALL NIGHT IT BULLIED YOU"

All night it bullied you.
When it shook you hard enough
They took you away.
I was shaken too. I walked
The frantic corridor praying
Representing
My terror so minutely
It went unnoticed.

The whole place moaned
As it was meant to.
A door flung out a nurse and a scream.
A doctor in a butcher's apron passed
Tying his gauze.
The nurse returned with forceps.

Your door stayed shut. I smoked.
You might have been dead. Or sleeping.

Bloodshot and drugged you burbled about our boy.
He frothed, mildly confronting whatever it was
Flooded his lungs. I was full of pieties.
We had never been so nearly anonymous.

C. K. STEAD

From "A Small Registry of Births and Deaths"

ON A BIRTH

Is it a happiness?
Yew branches flog the air,
Occasionally a white flake
Comes largely down.
Stitched and torn, who is
My child sleeps deeply
In another town. A wet child
Was drawn from her by
Its feet.
     It wavers here,
Here wavers to sleet.

A happiness?
     A genetic string
So far is incomplete.
Another infant has begun
Another web of living, fine
Branches of a lung.
(On TV I saw the skin
Held back: from outside eager
Pulsations of an infant's
Baglike lung.) In happiness
What my child willed
Is done.

GEOFFREY GRIGSON

53

TO LUCIA AT BIRTH

Though the moon beaming matronly and bland
   Greets you, among the crowd of the new-born,
With "welcome to the world" yet understand
   That still her pale, lascivious unicorn
And bloody lion are loose on either hand:
   With din of bones and tantarará of horn
Their fanciful cortège parades the land—
   Pest on the high road, wild-fire in the corn.

Outrageous company to be born into,
   Lunatics of a royal age long dead.
Then reckon time by what you are or do,
   Not by the epochs of the war they spread.
   Hark how they roar; but never turn your head.
Nothing will change them, let them not change you.

ROBERT GRAVES

NINTH MONTH

For weeks, now months, the year in burden goes,
a happiness so slow burning, it is lasting;
our animated nettles are black slash
by August. Today I leaned through lunch on my elbows,
watching my nose bleed red lacquer on the grass;
I see, smell and taste blood in everything–
I almost imagine your experience mine.
This year by miracle, you've jumped from 38
to 40, joined your elders who can judge:
woman has never forgiven man her blood.

Sometimes the indictment dies in your forgetting.
You move on crutches into your ninth month,
you break things now almost globular—
love in your fullness of flesh and heart and humor.

ROBERT LOWELL
From "Marriage", Stanza 11

ROBERT SHERIDAN LOWELL

Your midnight ambulances, the first knife-saw
of the child, feet-first, a string of tobacco tied
to your throat that won't go down, your window heaped
with brown paper bags leaking peaches and avocados,
your meals tasting like Kleenex . . . too much blood is
    seeping . . .
after twelve hours of labor to come out right,
in less than thirty seconds swimming the blood-flood:
Little Gingersnap Man, homoform,
flat and sore and alcoholic red,
only like us in owning to middle-age.
"If you touch him, he'll burn your fingers."
"It's his health, not fever. Why are the other babies so
    pallid?
His navy-blue eyes tip with his head. . . . Darling,
we have escaped our death-struggle with our lives."

ROBERT LOWELL
From "Marriage", Stanza 13

OVERHANGING CLOUD

This morning the overhanging clouds are piecrust,
milelong Luxor Temples based on rich runny ooze;
my old life settles down into the archives.
It's strange having a child today, though common,
adding our further complication to
intense fragility.
Clouds go from dull to dazzle all the morning;
we have not grown as our child did in the womb,
met Satan like Milton going blind in London;
it's enough to wake without old fears,
and watch the needle-fire of the first light
bombarding off your eyelids harmlessly.
By ten the bedroom is sultry. You have double-breathed;
we are many, our bed smells of hay.

ROBERT LOWELL
From "Marriage", Stanza 14

HELLO

Hello there, Biscuit! You're a better-looking broad
by much than, and your sister's dancing up & down.
"I just gave one mighty Push"
your mother says, and we are all in business.

I thought your mother might powder my knuckles
gript at one point, with wild eyes on my tie
"Don't move!" and then the screams began,
they wheeled her off, and we are all in business.

56

I wish I knew what business (son) we're in
I can't wait seven weeks to see her grin
I'm not myself, we are all changing here
direction *and* velocity, to   accommodate you, dear.

JOHN BERRYMAN

THE MAGUS

It is time for the others to come.
This child is no more than a god.

No cars are moving this night.
The lights in the houses go out.

I put these out with the rest.
From his crib, the child begins

To shine, letting forth one ray
Through the twelve simple bars of his bed

Down into the trees, where two
Long-lost other men shall be drawn

Slowly up to the brink of the house,
Slowly in through the breath on the window.

But how did I get in this room?
Is this my son, or another's?

Where is the woman to tell me
How my face is lit up by his body?

It is time for the others to come.
An event more miraculous yet

Is the thing I am shining to tell you.
This child is no more than a child.

JAMES DICKEY

"DEAR CHILD WHOM I BEGOT"

Dear child whom I begot,
Forgive me if my page
Hymns not your helpless age,
For you are mine, and not:
Mine as sower and sown,
But in yourself your own.

J. V. CUNNINGHAM

CRADLE SONG

Erce . . . Erce . . . Erce
Primigravida

curled like a hoop in sleep
unearthly of manufacture,
tissue of blossom and clay
bone the extract of air
fountain of nature.

softly knitted by kisses,
added to stitch by stitch,
by sleep of the dying heart,
by water and wool and air,
gather a fabric rich.

earth contracted to earth
in ten toes: the cardinals.
in ten fingers: the bishops.
ears by two, eyes by two,
watch the mirror watching you,

and now hush

the nightwalkers bringing peace,
seven the badges of grace
five the straw caps of talent,
one the scarf of desire, go
mimic your mother's lovely face.

LAWRENCE DURRELL

BIRTH

Oh, fields of wonder
Out of which
Stars are born,
And moon and sun
And me as well,
Like stroke
Of lightning
In the night
Some mark
To make
Some word
To tell.

LANGSTON HUGHES

THE BIRTHNIGHT: TO F.

[The poet's daughter, Florence]

Dearest, it was a night
That in its darkness rocked Orion's stars;
A sighing wind ran faintly white
Along the willows, and the cedar boughs
Laid their wide hands in stealthy peace across
The starry silence of their antique moss:
No sound save rushing air
Cold, yet all sweet with Spring,
And in thy mother's arms, couched weeping there,
     Thou, lovely thing.

WALTER DE LA MARE

THE LITTLE BIRD

My dear Daddie bought a mansion
    For to bring my Mammie to,
In a hat with a long feather,
    And a trailing gown of blue;
And a company of fiddlers
    And a rout of maids and men
Danced the clock round to the morning,
    In a gay house-warming then.
And when all the guests were gone—and
    All was still as still can be,
In from the dark ivy hopped a
    Wee small bird. And that was Me.

WALTER DE LA MARE

SATURDAY'S CHILD

Some are teethed on a silver spoon,
    With the stars strung for a rattle;
I cut my teeth as the black raccoon—
    For implements of battle.

Some are swaddled in silk and down,
    And heralded by a star;
They swathed my limbs in a sackcloth gown
    On a night that was black as tar.

For some, godfather and goddame
    The opulent fairies be;
Dame Poverty gave me my name,
    And Pain godfathered me.

For I was born on Saturday—
    "Bad time for planting a seed,"
Was all my father had to say,
    And, "One mouth more to feed."

Death cut the strings that gave me life,
    And handed me to Sorrow,
The only kind of middle wife
    My folks could beg or borrow.

COUNTEE CULLEN

INFANT JOY

"I have no name:
"I am but two days old."
What shall I call thee?
"I happy am,
"Joy is my name."
Sweet joy befall thee!

Pretty joy!
Sweet joy but two days old,
Sweet joy I call thee:
Thou dost smile,
I sing the while,
Sweet joy befall thee!

WILLIAM BLAKE
From *Songs of Innocence*

INFANT SORROW

My mother groan'd! my father wept.
Into the dangerous world I leapt:
Helpless, naked, piping loud:
Like a fiend hid in a cloud.

Struggling in my father's hands,
Striving against my swadling bands,
Bound and weary I thought best
To sulk upon my mother's breast.

WILLIAM BLAKE
From *Songs of Experience*

BABY SONG

From the private ease of Mother's womb
I fall into the lighted room.

Why don't they simply put me back
Where it is warm and wet and black?

But one thing follows on another.
Things were different inside Mother.

Padded and jolly I would ride
The perfect comfort of her inside.

They tuck me in a rustling bed
—I lie there, raging, small, and red.

I may sleep soon, I may forget,
But I won't forget that I regret.

A rain of blood poured round her womb,
But all time roars outside this room.

THOM GUNN

WAR-BABY

The child like mustard seed
Rolls out of the husk of death
    Into the woman's fertile, fathomless lap

Look, it has taken root!
See how it flourisheth!
    See how it rises with magical, rosy sap!

As for our faith, it was there
When we did not know, did not care;
    It fell from our husk in a little hasty seed.

Say, is it all we need?
Is it true that the little weed
    Will flourish its branches in heaven when we
      slumber beneath?

D. H. LAWRENCE

ECCE PUER

[On the birth of his grandson after his own father's death]

Of the dark past
A child is born;
With joy and grief
My heart is torn.

Calm in his cradle
The living lies.
May love and mercy
Unclose his eyes!

Young life is breathed
On the glass;
The world that was not
Comes to pass.

A child is sleeping:
An old man gone.
O, father forsaken,
Forgive your son!

JAMES JOYCE

BIRTH REPORT

When blam! my father's gun began the dash
Of fifty thousand tadpoles for one egg,
I set myself without a leg to leg
Like sixty for the tape. A tungsten flash,
And then my mother in a nest my aunt
Had paid for let me down.

                      How can so short
A time have worn so dim the birth report
White, Anglo-Saxon, one-half Protestant?

X. J. KENNEDY
From "Snapshots"

THE EVIL EYE

*[The belief in the Evil Eye is a still-surviving superstition among Italian
peasants. One method of detecting its presence is to pour olive oil
on a saucer of holy water. The shapes assumed by the oil can then
be read by the gifted.]*

Nona poured oil on the water and saw the eye
    form on my birth. Zia beat me with bay
    fennel and barley to scourge the devil away.
I doubt I needed so much excuse to cry.

From Sister Maria Immaculata there came
    a crucifix, a vow of nine days' prayer,
    a scapular stitched with virgin's hair.
The eye glowed on the water all the same.

By Felicia, the midwife, I was hung with a tin
    fish stuffed with garlic and bread crumbs.
    Three holy waters washed the breast for my gums.
Still the eye glared, wide as original sin

on the deepest pools of women midnight-spoken
    to ward my clamoring soul from the clutch of hell,
    lest growing I be no comfort and dying swell
more than a grave with horror. Still unbroken

the eye glared through the roosts of all their clucking.
    "Jesu," cried Mother, "why is he deviled so?"
    "Baptism without delay," said Father Cosmo.
"This one is not for sprinkling but for ducking."

So in came meat and wine and the feast was on.
    I wore a palm frond in my lace, and sewn
    to my swaddling band a hoop and three beads of bone
for the Trinity. And they ducked me and called me John.

And ate the meat and drank the wine, and the eye
    closed on the water. All this fell between
    my first scream and first name in 1916,
the year of the war and the influenza, when I

was not yet ready for evil or my own name,
though I had one already and the other came.

JOHN CIARDI

IN THE FLEETING HAND OF TIME

On the steps of the bright madhouse
I hear the bearded bell shaking down the woodlawn
the final knell of my world
I climb and enter a fiery gathering of knights
they unaware of my presence lay forth sheepskin plans
and with mailcoated fingers trace my arrival
back back back when on the black steps of Nero lyre
                                        Rome I stood

in my arms the wailing philosopher
the final call of mad history
Now my presence is known
my arrival marked by illuminated stains
The great windows of Paradise open
Down to radiant dust fall the curtains of Past Time
In fly flocks of multicolored birds
Light winged light O the wonder of light
Time takes me by the hand
born March 26 1930 I am led 100 mph o'er the vast
                                        market of choice

what to choose? what to choose?
Oh—and I leave my orange room of myth
no chance to lock away my toys of Zeus
I choose the room of Bleecker Street
A baby mother stuffs my mouth with a pale Milanese
                                        breast

I suck I struggle I cry O Olympian mother
unfamiliar this breast to me
Snows
Decade of icy asphalt doomed horses
Weak dreams   Dark corridors of P.S.42   Roofs
                                Ratthroated pigeons

Led 100 mph over these all too real Mafia streets
profanely I shed my Hermean wings

O Time be merciful
throw me beneath your humanity of cars
feed me to giant grey skyscrapers
exhaust my heart to your bridges
I discard my lyre of Orphic futility

And for such betrayal I climb these bright mad steps
and enter this room of paradiscal light
ephemeral
Time
a long long dog having chased its orbited tail
comes grab my hand
and leads me into conditional life

GREGORY CORSO

TRUE CONFESSIONAL

I was conceived in the summer of Nineteen Eighteen
(or was it Thirty Eight)
when some kind of war was going on
but it didn't stop two people
from making love in Ossining that year
I like to think on a riverbank in sun
On a picnic by the Hudson
as in a painting of the Hudson River School
or up at Bear Mountain maybe
after taking the old Hudson River Line
paddlewheel excursion steamer
(I may have added the paddlewheel—
the Hudson my Mississippi)

And on the way back she
already carried me
inside of her
I lawrence ferlinghetti
wrought from the dark in my mother long ago
born in a small back bedroom—
In the next room my brother heard
the first cry,
many years later wrote me—
"Poor Mom—No husband—No money—Pop dead—
How she went through it all—"
Someone squeezed my heart
to make it go
I cried and sprang up
Open eye open heart where
do I wander
I cried and ran off
into the heart of the world
Carried away
by another I knew not
And which of me shall know my brother?
"I am my son, my mother, my father,
I am born of myself
my own flesh sucked"
And someone squeezed my heart
to make me go
And I began to go
through my number
I was a wind-up toy
someone had dropped wound-up
into a world already
running down
The world had been going on
a long time already
but it made no difference
It was new it was like new

i made it new
i saw it shining
and it shone in the sun
and it spun in the sun
and the skein it spun
was pure light
My life was made of it
made of the skeins of light
The cobwebs of Night
were not on it
were not of it
It was too bright
to see
too luminous
to cast a shadow
and there was another world
behind the bright screens
I had only to close my eyes
for another world to appear
too near and too dear
to be anything but myself
my inside self
where everything real
was to happen
in this place which still exists
inside myself
and hasn't changed that much
certainly not as much
as the outside
with its bag of skin
and its "aluminum beard"
and its blue blue eyes
which see as one eye
in the middle of the head
where everything happens
except what happens

in the heart
vajra lotus diamond heart
wherein I read
the poem that never ends
LAWRENCE FERLINGHETTI

THE BIRTH IN A NARROW ROOM

Weeps out of western country something new.
Blurred and stupendous. Wanted and unplanned.
    Winks. Twines, and weakly winks
Upon the milk-glass fruit bowl, iron pot,
The bashful china child tipping forever
Yellow apron and spilling pretty cherries.

Now, weeks and years will go before she thinks
"How pinchy is my room! how can I breathe!
I am not anything and I have got
Not anything, or anything to do!"—
But prances nevertheless with gods and fairies
Blithely about the pump and then beneath
The elms and grapevines, then in darling endeavor
By privy foyer, where the screenings stand
And where the bugs buzz by in private cars
Across old peach cans and old jelly jars.

GWENDOLYN BROOKS

CRADLE SONG FOR MIRIAM

The clock's untiring fingers wind the wool of darkness
And we all lie alone, having long outgrown our cradles
(Sleep, sleep, Miriam)
And the flames like faded ladies always unheeded simper
And all is troubledness.

Soft the wool, dark the wool
Is gathered slowly, wholly up
Into a ball, all of it.

And yet in the back of the mind, lulled all else.
There is something unsleeping, un-tamperable-with
Something that whines and scampers
And like the ladies in the grate will not sleep nor forget
     itself,
Clawing at the wool like a kitten.

Sleep, sleep, Miriam.
And as for this animal of yours
He must be cradled also.
That he may not unravel this handiwork of forgetfulness,
·That he may not philander with the flames before they
     die.

The world like a cradle rises and falls
On a wave of confetti and funerals
And sordor and stinks and stupid faces
And the deity making bored grimaces.

Oh what a muddle he has made of the wool,
(God will tomorrow have his hands full),
You must muzzle your beast, you must fasten him
For the whole of life—the interim.

Through the interim we pass
Everyone under an alias
Till they gather the strands of us together
And wind us up for ever and ever.

The clock's fingers wind, wind the wool of Lethe,
(Sleep, sleep, Miriam)
It glides across the floor drawn by hidden fingers
And the beast droops his head
And the fire droops its flounces
And winks a final ogle out of the fading embers
But no one pays attention;

This is too much, the flames say, insulted,
We who were once the world's beauties and now
No one pays attention
No one remembers us.

LOUIS MACNEICE

UNKNOWN GIRL IN THE MATERNITY WARD

Child, the current of your breath is six days long.
You lie, a small knuckle on my white bed;
lie, fisted like a snail, so small and strong
at my breast. Your lips are animals; you are fed
with love. At first hunger is not wrong.
The nurses nod their caps; you are shepherded
down starch halls with the other unnested throng
in wheeling baskets. You tip like a cup; your head
moving to my touch. You sense the way we belong.
But this is an institution bed.
You will not know me very long.

74

The doctors are enamel. They want to know
the facts. They guess about the man who left me,
some pendulum soul, going the way men go
and leave you full of child. But our case history
stays blank. All I did was let you grow.
Now we are here for all the ward to see.
They thought I was strange, although
I never spoke a word. I burst empty
of you, letting you learn how the air is so.
The doctors chart the riddle they ask of me
and I turn my head away. I do not know.

Yours is the only face I recognize.
Bone at my bone, you drink my answers in.
Six times a day I prize
your need, the animals of your lips, your skin
growing warm and plump. I see your eyes
lifting their tents. They are blue stones, they begin
to outgrow their moss. You blink in surprise
and I wonder what you can see, my funny kin,
as you trouble my silence. I am a shelter of lies.
Should I learn to speak again, or hopeless in
such sanity will I touch some face I recognize?

Down the hall the baskets start back. My arms
fit you like a sleeve, they hold
catkins of your willows, the wild bee farms
of your nerves, each muscle and fold
of your first days. Your old man's face disarms
the nurses. But the doctors return to scold
me. I speak. It is you my silence harms.
I should have known; I should have told
them something to write down. My voice alarms
my throat. "Name of father—none." I hold
you and name you bastard in my arms.

And now that's that. There is nothing more
that I can say or lose.
Others have traded life before
and could not speak. I tighten to refuse
your owling eyes, my fragile visitor.
I touch your cheeks, like flowers. You bruise
against me. We unlearn. I am a shore
rocking you off. You break from me. I choose
your only way, my small inheritor
and hand you off, trembling the selves we lose.
Go child, who is my sin and nothing more.

ANNE SEXTON

TO C.F.H. ON HER CHRISTENING-DAY

Fair Caroline, I wonder what
You think of earth as a dwelling-spot,
And if you'd rather have come, or not?

Today has laid on you a name
That, though unasked for, you will claim
Lifelong, for love or praise or blame.

May chance and change impose on you
No heavier burthen than this new
Care-chosen one your future through!

Dear stranger here, the prayer is mine
That your experience may combine
Good things with glad. . . . Yes, Caroline!

THOMAS HARDY

I MET THIS GUY WHO DIED
For J.L.K. [Jean-Louis (Jack) Kerouac]

We caroused
    did the bars
        became fast friends
He wanted me to tell him
    what poetry was
        I told him

Happy tipsy one night
I took him home to see my newborn child
A great sorrow overcame him
"O Gregory" he moaned
        "you brought up something to die"

GREGORY CORSO

THE SON

It was your mother wanted you;
you were already half-formed
when I entered. But can I deny
the hunger, the loneliness bringing me in
from myself? And when you appeared
before me, there was no repentance
for what I had done, as there was shame
in the doing it; compassion only
for that which was too small to be called
human. The unfolding of your hands

77

was plant-like, your ear was the shell
I thundered in; your cries, when they came,
were those of a blind creature
trodden upon; pain not yet become grief.

R. S. THOMAS

A POET'S WELCOME TO HIS LOVE-BEGOTTEN DAUGHTER; THE FIRST INSTANCE THAT ENTITLED HIM TO THE VENERABLE APPELLATION OF FATHER—

Thou's welcome, Wean! Mischanter fa' me,
If thoughts o' thee, or yet thy Mamie,
Shall ever daunton me or awe me,
   My bonie lady;
Or if I blush when thou shalt ca' me
   Tyta, or Daddie.—

Tho' now they ca' me, Fornicator,
And tease my name in kintra clatter,
The mair they talk, I'm kend the better;
   E'en let them clash!
An auld wife's tongue's a feckless matter
   To gie ane fash.—

Welcome! My bonie, sweet, wee Dochter!
Tho' ye come here a wee unsought for;
And tho' your comin I hae fought for,
   Baith Kirk and Queir;
Yet by my faith, ye're no unwrought for,
   That I shall swear!

Wee image o' my bonie Betty,
As fatherly I kiss and daut thee,
As dear and near my heart I set thee,
   Wi' as gude will,
As a' the Priests had seen me get thee
   That's out o' h—.—

Sweet fruit o' monie a merry dint,
My funny toil is no a' tint;
Tho' ye come to the warld asklent,
   Which fools may scoff at,
In my last plack your part's be in't,
   The better half o't.—

Tho' I should be the waur bestead,
Thou's be as braw and bienly clad,
And thy young years as nicely bred
   Wi' education,
As ony brat o' Wedlock's bed,
   In a' thy station.—

(Lord grant that thou may ay inherit
Thy Mither's looks an' gracefu' merit;
An' thy poor, worthless Daddie's spirit,
   Without his failins!
'Twad please me mair to see thee heir it
   Than stocked mailins!)

For if thou be, what I wad hae thee,
And tak the counsel I shall gie thee,
I'll never rue my trouble wi' thee,
   The cost nor shame o't,
But be a loving Father to thee,
   And brag the name o't.—
      ROBERT BURNS

THE RITE

For nine months
I watched my speck of love
enlarge and grow enormous
in the great lens of your belly
till your sleep was broken
on the obstacle in your lap.

You wanted me
to watch you giving birth,
you said it was a bond between us
your body labouring.
But I knew my work would take me
two hundred miles away that week.

Unable to help
watching pain cram your loins
I'd stand by
cornered in our cramped room
taking your pulse in the doctor's way
and dear you softly as you choked
for gas, not air.

Your fingers
in their pain clutching my wrist
would gain a hold on me
I could not wrest away in dreams or rows.
The butting head that splits you
bears features I once had.

Initiate
of a secret society now
your murmur parturition rites I cannot know,
the breaking of the waters.
And tonight you rest these miles distant;
your time about my wrist.

                                        PETER DALE

THE VISIBLE BABY

A large transparent baby like a skeleton in a red tree,
Like a little skeleton in the rootlet-pattern;
He is not of glass, this baby, his flesh is see-through,
Otherwise he is quite the same as any other baby.

I can see the white caterpillar of his milk looping through
                                                    him,
I can see the pearl-bubble of his wind and stroke it out of
                                                    him,
I can see his little lungs breathing like pink parks of trees,
I can see his little brain in its glass case like a budding
                                                    rose;

There are his teeth in his transparent gums like a budding
                                                    hawthorn twig,
His eyes like open poppies follow the light,
His tongue is like a crest of his thumping blood,
His heart like two squirrels one scarlet, one purple
Mating in the canopy of a blood-tree;

His spine like a necklace, all silvery-strung with cartilages,
His handbones like a working-party of white insects,
His nerves like a tree of ice with sunlight shooting
                                                    through it,

What a closed book bound in wrinkled illustration his
                                            father is to him!
                                            PETER REDGROVE

ON THE "SIEVERING" TRAM

Square figures climb off and on;
mufflers, Astrakhan hats.
A wintry night for a ride to a clinic
to visit a new-born boy and his mother;
and the bell hurrah-ing.

Too many life-bullied faces
packed on the Sievering tram.
Yet a woman smiles at a baby near her
and beckons and beckons, as we run lurch
-ing, and sigh and restart.

That baby views the woman steadily;
(and the floor is all mucked with snow.)
What do I bring to the boy and his mother
lying in the clinic? Daffodils,
bewilderment and love,

Ready money, a clock and a signature.
A Neon-light Pegasus glows in the sky
(Somebody's Oil) as we swing corners
past bakers' and laundries and snow, with the traffic
-gongs ringing like glory.

BERNARD SPENCER

ON THE BIRTH OF DAN GOLDMAN
A Song of Triumph

[Written in 1968 while in prison for anti-Vietnam war activities. Berrigan and the Goldmans were friends from Cornell.]

my 50th year having arrived
and striding so to speak the heights—
i.e., recently appointed
Laureate In Residence At The Imperial Madhouse,
Woebegone Acres.   Duties: the striking
of dawn and twilight fires, incantations,
communalities, observances,
a spartan rigor, open air,
work, study, prescience of stern eyes

well   on a certain dawn like any
other dawn   (dawn here being dusk
inside out;   the whole
backward   forward
a single fabric
woven by mad   fingers   under which
freudian legerdemain makes
bad miracles   remorse   sour tears)

a birth!
in this landlocked hell   a dove bore
in his beak   a missive
scrawled in a day-old hand
dropped   a flower at my feet
it cried   or the dove cried   or the child
I am born! born!

and I could not believe it and
was thereby confirmed a man
whose birth his parents
for very joy   theirs their parents
and so on
could not believe

the closing of eyes
being much more our skill
than raising like a wineglass
the bloodied child for a blessing

I must tell (the telling
hurts like his mother's wound
his father's passion   compassion)
Jack, Beatrice, parents
I hear this little boy Dan
pipe like a lamb   *God is my judge*
one hand in his mother's   one
in his father's hand   he withstands
the mechanical bullies of the world
death   the undoer of children

Jailhouse   underground
the stinking alleys   fair Ithaca
the slave farms   fair Cornell
the poor languish   die by decree
those fields of combat
where cowards dread show face—

No, fields of joy!   a child's
metaphysical purity dawns
on the befouled world
parents   strangers   friends
Philip and you and I and
the cheated Asian children
first breath wrung from last
all   all are drawn, all
born, twice born, solve
resolve the mystical dance.

DANIEL BERRIGAN

THREE WOMEN
A POEM FOR THREE VOICES

Setting: A maternity ward and round about

FIRST VOICE:
I am slow as the world. I am very patient,
Turning through my time, the suns and stars
Regarding me with attention.
The moon's concern is more personal:
She passes and repasses, luminous as a nurse.
Is she sorry for what will happen? I do not think so.
She is simply astonished at fertility.

When I walk out, I am a great event.
I do not have to think, or even rehearse.
What happens in me will happen without attention.
The pheasant stands on the hill;
He is arranging his brown feathers.
I cannot help smiling at what it is I know.
Leaves and petals attend me. I am ready.

SECOND VOICE:
When I first saw it, the small red seep, I did not believe it.
I watched the men walk about me in the office. They were
    so flat!
There was something about them like cardboard, and now
    I had caught it,
That flat, flat, flatness from which ideas, destructions,
Bulldozers, guillotines, white chambers of shrieks proceed,
Endlessly proceed—and the cold angels, the abstractions.
I sat at my desk in my stockings, my high heels.

And the man I work for laughed: "Have you seen
    something awful?
You are so white, suddenly." And I said nothing.
I saw death in the bare trees, a deprivation.
I could not believe it. Is it so difficult
For the spirit to conceive a face, a mouth?
The letters proceed from these black keys, and these black
    keys proceed
From my alphabetical fingers, ordering parts.

Parts, bits, cogs, the shining multiples.
I am dying as I sit. I lose a dimension.
Trains roar in my ears, departures, departures!
The silver track of time empties into the distance,
The white sky empties of its promise, like a cup.
These are my feet, these mechanical echoes.
Tap, tap, tap, steel pegs. I am found wanting.

This is a disease I carry home, this is a death.
Again, this is a death. Is it the air,
The particles of destruction I suck up? Am I a pulse
That wanes and wanes, facing the cold angel?
Is this my lover then? This death, this death?
As a child I loved a lichen-bitten name.
Is this the one sin then, this old dead love of death?

THIRD VOICE:
I remember the minute when I knew for sure.
The willows were chilling,
The face in the pool was beautiful, but not mine—
It had a consequential look, like everything else,
And all I could see was dangers: doves and words,
Stars and showers of gold—conceptions, conceptions!
I remember a white, cold wing

And the great swan, with its terrible look,
Coming at me, like a castle, from the top of the river.
There is a snake in swans.
He glided by; his eye had a black meaning.
I saw the world in it—small, mean and black,
Every little word hooked to every little word, and act to
    act.
A hot blue day had budded into something.

I wasn't ready. The white clouds rearing
Aside were dragging me in four directions.
I wasn't ready.
I had no reverence.
I thought I could deny the consequence—
But it was too late for that. It was too late, and the face
Went on shaping itself with love, as if I was ready.

SECOND VOICE:
It is a world of snow now. I am not at home.
How white these sheets are. The faces have no features.
They are bald and impossible, like the faces of my children,
Those little sick ones that elude my arms.
Other children do not touch me: they are terrible.
They have too many colours, too much life. They are not
    quiet,
Quiet, like the little emptinesses I carry.

I have had my chances. I have tried and tried.
I have stitched life into me like a rare organ,
And walked carefully, precariously, like something rare.
I have tried not to think too hard. I have tried to be
    natural.
I have tried to be blind in love, like other women,
Blind in my bed, with my dear blind sweet one,
Not looking, through the thick dark, for the face of
    another.

I did not look. But still the face was there,
The face of the unborn one that loved its perfections,
The face of the dead one that could only be perfect
In its easy peace, could only keep holy so.
And then there were other faces. The faces of nations,
Governments, parliaments, societies,
The faceless faces of important men.

It is these men I mind:
They are so jealous of anything that is not flat! They are
   jealous gods
That would have the whole world flat because they are.
I see the Father conversing with the Son.
Such flatness cannot but be holy.
"Let us make a heaven," they say.
"Let us flatten and launder the grossness from these souls."

FIRST VOICE:
I am calm. I am calm. It is the calm before something
   awful:
The yellow minute before the wind walks, when the leaves
Turn up their hands, their pallors. It is so quiet here.
The sheets, the faces, are white and stopped, like clocks.
Voices stand back and flatten. Their visible hieroglyphs
Flatten to parchment screens to keep the wind off.
They paint such secrets in Arabic, Chinese!

I am dumb and brown. I am a seed about to break.
The brownness is my dead self, and it is sullen:
It does not wish to be more, or different.
Dusk hoods me in blue now, like a Mary.
O colour of distance and forgetfulness!—
When will it be, the second when Time breaks
And eternity engulfs it, and I drown utterly?

I talk to myself, myself only, set apart—
Swabbed and lurid with disinfectants, sacrificial.
Waiting lies heavy on my lids. It lies like sleep,
Like a big sea. Far off, far off, I feel the first wave tug
Its cargo of agony toward me, inescapable, tidal.
And I, a shell, echoing on this white beach
Face the voices that overwhelm, the terrible element.

THIRD VOICE:

I am a mountain now, among mountainy women.
The doctors move among us as if our bigness
Frightened the mind. They smile like fools.
They are to blame for what I am, and they know it.
They hug their flatness like a kind of health.
And what if they found themselves surprised, as I did?
They would go mad with it.

And what if two lives leaked between my thighs?
I have seen the white clean chamber with its instruments.
It is a place of shrieks. It is not happy.
"This is where you will come when you are ready."
The night lights are flat red moons. They are dull with
    blood.
I am not ready for anything to happen.
I should have murdered this, that murders me.

FIRST VOICE:

There is no miracle more cruel than this
I am dragged by the horses, the iron hooves.
I last. I last it out. I accomplish a work.
Dark tunnel, through which hurtle the visitations,
The visitations, the manifestations, the startled faces.
I am the centre of an atrocity.
What pains, what sorrows must I be mothering?

Can such innocence kill and kill? It milks my life.
The trees wither in the street. The rain is corrosive.
I taste it on my tongue, and the workable horrors,
The horrors that stand and idle, the slighted godmothers
With their hearts that tick and tick, with their satchel of
    instruments.
I shall be a wall and a roof, protecting.
I shall be a sky and a hill of good: O let me be!

A power is growing on me, an old tenacity.
I am breaking apart like the world. There is this blackness,
This ram of blackness. I fold my hands on a mountain.
The air is thick. It is thick with this working.
I am used. I am drummed into use.
My eyes are squeezed by this blackness.
I see nothing.

SECOND VOICE:
I am accused. I dream of massacres.
I am a garden of black and red agonies. I drink them,
Hating myself, hating and fearing. And now the world
    conceives
Its end and runs toward it, arms held out in love.
It is a love of death that sickens everything.
A dead sun stains the newsprint. It is red.
I lose life after life. The dark earth drinks them.

She is the vampire of us all. So she supports us,
Fattens us, is kind. Her mouth is red.
I know her, I know her intimately—
Old winter-face, old barren one, old time bomb.
Men have used her meanly. She will eat them.
Eat them, eat them, eat them in the end.
The sun is down. I die. I make a death.

FIRST VOICE:
Who is he, this blue, furious boy,
Shiny and strange, as if he had hurtled from a star?
He is looking so angrily!
He flew into the room, a shriek at his heel.
The blue colour pales. He is human after all.
A red lotus opens in its bowl of blood;
They are stitching me up with silk, as if I were a material.

What did my fingers do before they held him?
What did my heart do, with its love?
I have never seen a thing so clear.
His lids are like the lilac-flower
And soft as a moth, his breath.
I shall not let go.
There is no guile or warp in him. May he keep so.

SECOND VOICE:
There is the moon in the high window. It is over.
How winter fills my soul! And that chalk light
Laying its scales on the windows, the windows of empty
    offices,
Empty schoolrooms, empty churches. O so much
    emptiness!
There is this cessation. This terrible cessation of everything.
These bodies mounded around me now, these polar
    sleepers—
What blue, moony ray ices their dreams?

I feel it enter me, cold, alien, like an instrument.
And that mad, hard face at the end of it, that O-mouth
Open in its gape of perpetual grieving.
It is she that drags the blood-black sea around
Month after month, with its voices of failure.
I am helpless as the sea at the end of her string.
I am restless. Restless and useless. I, too, create corpses.

I shall move north. I shall move into a long blackness.
I see myself as a shadow, neither man nor woman,
Neither a woman, happy to be like a man, nor a man
Blunt and flat enough to feel no lack. I feel a lack.
I hold my fingers up, ten white pickets.
See, the darkness is leaking from the cracks.
I cannot contain it. I cannot contain my life.

I shall be a heroine of the peripheral.
I shall not be accused by isolate buttons,
Holes in the heels of socks, the white mute faces
Of unanswered letters, coffined in a letter case.
I shall not be accused, I shall not be accused.
The clock shall not find me wanting, nor these stars
That rivet in place abyss after abyss.

THIRD VOICE:
I see her in my sleep, my red, terrible girl.
She is crying through the glass that separates us.
She is crying, and she is furious.
Her cries are hooks that catch and grate like cats.
It is by these hooks she climbs to my notice.
She is crying at the dark, or at the stars
That at such a distance from us shine and whirl.

I think her little head is carved in wood,
A red, hard wood, eyes shut and mouth wide open.
And from the open mouth issue sharp cries
Scratching at my sleep like arrows,
Scratching at my sleep, and entering my side.
My daughter has no teeth. Her mouth is wide.
It utters such dark sounds it cannot be good.

FIRST VOICE:
What is it that flings these innocent souls at us?
Look, they are so exhausted, they are all flat out
In their canvas-sided cots, names tied to their wrists,
The little silver trophies they've come so far for.
There are some with thick black hair, there are some bald.
Their skin tints are pink or sallow, brown or red;
They are beginning to remember their differences.

I think they are made of water; they have no expression.
Their features are sleeping, like light on quiet water.
They are the real monks and nuns in their identical
    garments.
I see them showering like stars on to the world—
On India, Africa, America, these miraculous ones,
These pure, small images. They smell of milk.
Their footsoles are untouched. They are walkers of air.

Can nothingness be so prodigal?
Here is my son.
His wide eye is that general, flat blue.
He is turning to me like a little, blind, bright plant.
One cry. It is the hook I hang on.
And I am a river of milk.
I am a warm hill.

SECOND VOICE:
I am not ugly. I am even beautiful.
The mirror gives back a woman without deformity.
The nurses give back my clothes, and an identity.
It is usual, they say, for such a thing to happen.
It is usual in my life, and the lives of others.
I am one in five, something like that. I am not hopeless.
I am beautiful as a statistic. Here is my lipstick.

I draw on the old mouth.
The red mouth I put by with my identity
A day ago, two days, three days ago. It was a Friday.
I do not even need a holiday; I can go to work today.
I can love my husband, who will understand.
Who will love me through the blur of my deformity
As if I had lost an eye, a leg, a tongue.

And so I stand, a little sightless. So I walk
Away on wheels, instead of legs, they serve as well.
And learn to speak with fingers, not a tongue.
The body is resourceful.
The body of a starfish can grow back its arms
And newts are prodigal in legs. And may I be
As prodigal in what lacks me.

THIRD VOICE:
She is a small island, asleep and peaceful,
And I am a white ship hooting: Goodbye, goodbye.
The day is blazing. It is very mournful.
The flowers in this room are red and tropical.
They have lived behind glass all their lives, they have been
    cared for tenderly.
Now they face a winter of white sheets, white faces.
There is very little to go into my suitcase.

There are the clothes of a fat woman I do not know.
There is my comb and brush. There is an emptiness.
I am so vulnerable suddenly.
I am a wound walking out of hospital.
I am a wound that they are letting go.
I leave my health behind. I leave someone
Who would adhere to me: I undo her fingers like
    bandages:
I go.

I am myself again. There are no loose ends.
I am bled white as wax, I have no attachments.
I am flat and virginal, which means nothing has
  happened,
Nothing that cannot be erased, ripped up and scrapped,
  begun again.
These little black twigs do not think to bud,
Nor do these dry, dry gutters dream of rain.
This woman who meets me in windows—she is neat.

So neat she is transparent, like a spirit.
How shyly she superimposes her neat self
On the inferno of African oranges, the heel-hung pigs.
She is deferring to reality.
It is I. It is I—
Tasting the bitterness between my teeth.
The incalculable malice of the everyday.

How long can I be a wall, keeping the wind off?
How long can I be
Gentling the sun with the shade of my hand,
Intercepting the blue bolts of a cold moon?
The voices of loneliness, the voices of sorrow
Lap at my back ineluctably.
How shall it soften them, this little lullaby?

How long can I be a wall around my green property?
How long can my hands
Be a bandage to his hurt, and my words
Bright birds in the sky, consoling, consoling?
It is a terrible thing
To be so open: it is as if my heart
Put on a face and walked into the world.

THIRD VOICE:
Today the colleges are drunk with spring.
My black gown is a little funeral:
It shows I am serious.
The books I carry wedge into my side.
I had an old wound once, but it is healing.
I had a dream of an island, red with cries.
It was a dream, and did not mean a thing.

FIRST VOICE:
Dawn flowers in the great elm outside the house.
The swifts are back. They are shrieking like paper rockets.
I hear the sound of the hours
Widen and die in the hedgerows. I hear the moo of cows.
The colours replenish themselves, and the wet
Thatch smokes in the sun.
The narcissi open white faces in the orchard.

I am reassured. I am reassured.
These are the clear bright colours of the nursery,
The talking ducks, the happy lambs.
I am simple again. I believe in miracles.
I do not believe in those terrible children
Who injure my sleep with their white eyes, their fingerless
    hands.
They are not mine. They do not belong to me.

I shall meditate upon normality.
I shall meditate upon my little son.
He does not walk. He does not speak a word.
He is still swaddled in white bands.
But he is pink and perfect. He smiles so frequently.
I have papered his room with big roses,
I have painted little hearts on everything.

I do not will him to be exceptional.
It is the exception that interests the devil.
It is the exception that climbs the sorrowful hill
Or sits in the desert and hurts his mother's heart.
I will him to be common,
To love me as I love him,
And to marry what he wants and where he will.

THIRD VOICE:
Hot noon in the meadows. The buttercups
Swelter and melt, and the lovers
Pass by, pass by.
They are black and flat as shadows.
It is so beautiful to have no attachments!
I am solitary as grass. What is it I miss?
Shall I ever find it, whatever it is?

The swans are gone. Still the river
Remembers how white they were.
It strives after them with its lights.
It finds their shapes in a cloud.
What is that bird that cries
With such sorrow in its voice?
I am young as ever, it says. What is it I miss?

SECOND VOICE:
I am at home in the lamplight. The evenings are
    lengthening.
I am mending a silk slip: my husband is reading.
How beautifully the light includes these things.
There is a kind of smoke in the spring air,
A smoke that takes the parks, the little statues
With pinkness, as if a tenderness awoke,
A tenderness that did not tire, something healing.

I wait and ache. I think I have been healing.
There is a great deal else to do. My hands
Can stitch lace neatly on to this material. My husband
Can turn and turn the pages of a book.
And so we are at home together, after hours.
It is only time that weighs upon our hands.
It is only time, and that is not material.

The streets may turn to paper suddenly, but I recover
From the long fall, and find myself in bed,
Safe on the mattress, hands braced, as for a fall.
I find myself again. I am no shadow
Though there is a shadow starting from my feet. I am a
    wife.
The city waits and aches. The little grasses
Crack through stone, and they are green with life.

SYLVIA PLATH

Before Birth

Before Night

Now, until the break of day,
Through this house each fairy stray.
To the best bride-bed will we,
Which by us shall blessed be;
And the issue there create
Ever shall be fortunate.
So shall all the couples three
Ever true in loving be;
And the blots of Nature's hand
Shall not in their issue stand;
Never mole, hare lip, nor scar,
Nor mark prodigious, such as are
Despised in nativity,
Shall upon their children be.
With this field-dew consecrate,
Every fairy take his gait,
And each several chamber bless,
Through this palace, with sweet peace;
And the owner of it blest
Ever shall in safety rest.

WILLIAM SHAKESPEARE

From A *Midsummer Night's Dream*, Act 5, Scene 2

"WHO IS THE SAME, WHICH AT MY WINDOW PEEPES?"

Who is the same, which at my window peepes?
Or whose is that faire face, that shines so bright,
Is it not Cinthia, she that never sleepes,
But walkes about high heaven al the night?
O fayrest goddesse, do thou not envy
My love with me to spy:
For thou likewise didst love, though now unthought,
And for a fleece of woll, which privily,
The Latmian shephard once unto thee brought,
His pleasures with thee wrought.
Therefore to us be favorable now;
And sith of wemens labours thou hast charge,
And generation goodly dost enlarge,
Encline thy will t'effect our wishfull vow,
And the chast wombe informe with timely seed,
That may our comfort breed:
Till which we cease our hopefull hap to sing,
Ne let the woods us answere, nor our Eccho ring.

And thou great Juno, which with awful might
The lawes of the wedlock still dost patronize,
And the religion of the faith first plight
With sacred rites hast taught to solemnize:
And eeke for comfort often callèd art
Of women in their smart,
Eternally bind thou this lovely band,
And all thy blessings unto us impart.
And thou glad Genius, in whose gentle hand,
The bridale bowre and geniall bed remaine,
Without blemish or staine,
And the sweet pleasures of theyr loves delight
With secret ayde doest succour and supply,
Till they bring forth the fruitfull progeny,

Send us the timely fruit of this same night.
And thou fayre Hebe, and thou Hymen free,
Grant that it may so be.
Til which we cease your further prayse to sing,
Ne any woods shal answer, nor your Eccho ring.

And ye high heavens, the temple of the gods,
In which a thousand torches flaming bright
Doe burne, that to us wretched earthly clods,
In dreadful darknesse lend desirèd light;
And all ye powers which in the same remayne,
More then we men can fayne,
Poure out your blessing on us plentiously,
And happy influence upon us raine,
That we may raise a large posterity,
Which from the earth, which they may long possesse,
With lasting happinesse,
Up to your haughty pallaces may mount,
And for the guerdon of theyr glorious merit
May heavenly tabernacles there inherit,
Of blessed Saints for to increase the count.
So let us rest, sweet love, in hope of this,
And cease till then our tymely joyes to sing,
The woods no more us answer, nor our eccho ring.

EDMUND SPENSER
From "Epithalamion"

BEFORE THE BIRTH OF ONE OF
HER CHILDREN

All things within this fading world hath end,
Adversity doth still our joys attend;
No ties so strong, no friends so dear and sweet,
But with death's parting blow is sure to meet.
The sentence past is most irrevocable,
A common thing, yet oh inevitable.
How soon, my Dear, death may my steps attend,
How soon't may be thy Lot to lose thy friend,
We are both ignorant, yet love bids me
These farewell lines to recommend to thee,
That when that knot's untied that made us one,
I may seem thine, who in effect am none.
And if I see not half my dayes that's due,
What nature would, God grant to yours and you;
The many faults that well you know I have
Let be interr'd in my oblivious grave;
If any worth or virtue were in me,
Let that live freshly in thy memory
And when thou feel'st no grief, as I no harms,
Yet love thy dead, who long lay in thine arms.
And when thy loss shall be repaid with gains
Look to my little babes, my dear remains.
And if thou love thyself, or loved'st me,
These o protect from step Dames injury.
And if chance to thine eyes shall bring this verse,
With some sad sighs honour my absent Herse;
And kiss this paper for thy loves dear sake,
Who with salt tears this last Farewel did take.

ANNE BRADSTREET

BEING BORN IS IMPORTANT

Being born is important.
You who have stood at the bedposts
and seen a mother on her high harvest day,
the day of the most golden of harvest moons for her.

You who have seen the new wet child
dried behind the ears,
swaddled in soft fresh garments,
pursing its lips and sending a groping mouth
toward the nipples where white milk is ready—

You who have seen this love's payday
of wild toil and sweet agonizing—

You know being born is important.
You know nothing else was ever so important to you.
You understand the payday of love is so old,
So involved, so traced with circles of the moon,
So cunning with the secrets of the salts of the blood—
It must be older than the moon, older than salt.

CARL SANDBURG

BY THE BABE UNBORN

If trees were tall and grasses short,
   As in some crazy tale,
If here and there a sea were blue
   Beyond the breaking pale.

107

If a fixed fire hung in the air
    To warm me one day through,
If deep green hair grew on great hills,
    I know what I should do.

In dark I lie: dreaming that there
    Are great eyes cold or kind,
And twisted streets and silent doors,
    And living men behind.

Let storm-clouds come: better an hour,
    And leave to weep and fight,
Than all the ages I have ruled
    The empires of the night.

I think that if they gave me leave
    Within the world to stand,
I would be good through all the day
    I spent in fairyland.

They should not hear a word from me
    Of selfishness or scorn,
If only I could find the door,
    If only I were born.

                G. K. CHESTERTON

ANTE-NATAL DREAM

I only know that I was there
With hayseed in my hair
Lying on the shady side
Of a haycock in July.

A crowd was pressing round
My body on the ground
Prising the lids of my eyes—
Open and you'll be wise.

The sky that roared with bees,
The row of poplar trees
Along the stream struck deep
And would not let me sleep.

A boortree tried hard to
Let me see it grow,
Mere notice was enough,
She would take care of love.

A clump of nettles cried:
We'll saturate your pride
Till you are oozing with
The richness of our myth;

For we are all you'll know
No matter where you go—
Every insect, weed
Kept singing in my head.

Thistle, ragwort, bluebottle,
Cleg that maddens cattle
Were crowding round me there
With hayseed in my hair.

PATRICK KAVANAGH

THE EGGS

The bird with bone on the outside,
The smooth egg. Melt butter over your egg, let
The yolk shine in its clouds!

Once she poured clarified melted butter
On herself, so that she might shine
Like the moon, and remarked how she could turn

Round and round inside her buttered skin, and if
You take a handful of wet clay and press
A pip into it it becomes grapefruit,

But only if the seed awakes to your touch,
Only if you shine to the seed.
The morning after,

Her shine seemed gone, rainbowed off
In crowds of bathroom suds, relaxed
Over the warm and scented waterskin, but at breakfast

She smiled again like last night and the shine returned
To everything. She spread butter
Over her soldiers and dipped the strips

Of toast into hot egg, the shine
Broke out of that sealed egg, I swear it,
Like a radium of the kitchen (I saw

Our child shine before she was born:
In my dream I rubbed the best butter
Over the pregnant dome and as though

It were white paper windowing with the grease
The first thing that I saw was the smile
Of the babe looking out at me,

Her sucking thumb, and then how she
High up in the clear butter of her mother floated).

PETER REDGROVE

A SONG FOR SIMEON

Lord, the Roman hyacinths are blooming in bowls and
The winter sun creeps by the snow hills;
The stubborn season had made stand.
My life is light, waiting for the death wind,
Like a feather on the back of my hand.
Dust in sunlight and memory in corners
Wait for the wind that chills towards the dead land.

Grant us thy peace.
I have walked many years in this city,
Kept faith and fast, provided for the poor,
Have given and taken honour and ease.
There went never any rejected from my door.
Who shall remember my house, where shall live my
                                          children's children
When the time of sorrow is come?
They will take to the goat's path, and the fox's home,
Fleeing from the foreign faces and the foreign swords.

Before the time of cords and scourges and lamentation
Grant us thy peace.
Before the stations of the mountain of desolation,
Before the certain hour of maternal sorrow,
Now at this birth season of decease,
Let the Infant, the still unspeaking and unspoken Word,
Grant Israel's consolation
To one who has eighty years and no tomorrow.

According to thy word.
They shall praise Thee and suffer in every generation
With glory and derision,
Light upon light, mounting the saints' stair.
Not for me the martyrdom, the ecstasy of thought and
                                                      prayer,
Not for me the ultimate vision.
Grant me thy peace.
(And a sword shall pierce thy heart,
Thine also).
I am tired with my own life and the lives of those after
                                                      me,
I am dying in my own death and the deaths of those after
                                                      me.
Let thy servant depart,
Having seen thy salvation.

T. S. ELIOT

MOTHER

As I work at the pump, the wind heavy
With spits of rain is fraying
The rope of water I'm pumping.
It pays itself out like air's afterbirth
At each gulp of the plunger.

I am tired of the feeding of stock.
Each evening I labour this handle
Half an hour at a time, the cows
Guzzling at bowls in the byre.
Before I have topped up the level
They lower it down.

They've trailed in again by the readymade gate
He stuck into the fence: a jingling bedhead
Wired up between posts. It's on its last legs.
It does not jingle for joy any more.

I am tired of walking about with this plunger
Inside me. God, he plays like a young calf
Gone wild on a rope.
Lying or standing won't settle these capers,
This gulp in my well.

O when I am a gate for myself
Let such wind fray my waters
As scarfs my skirt through my thighs,
Stuffs air down my throat.

SEAMUS HEANEY

TO A CHILD BEFORE BIRTH

This summer is your perfect summer. Never will the skies
So stretched and strident be with blue
As these you do not see; never will the birds surprise
With such light flukes the ferns and fences
As these you do not hear. This year the may
Smells like rum-butter, and day by day
The petals slip from the cups like lovers' hands,
Tender and tired and satisfied. This year the haws
Will form as your fingers form, and when in August
The sun first stings your eyes,
The fruit will be red as brick and free to the throstles.
Oh but next year the may
Will have its old smell of plague about it; next year
The songs of the birds be selfish, the skies have rain;
Next year the apples will be tart again.
But do not always grieve
For the unseen summer. Perfection is not the land you
                                   leave,
It is the pole you measure from; it gives
Geography to your ways and wanderings.
What is your perfection is another's pain;
And because she in impossible season loves
So in her blood for you the bright bird sings.

NORMAN NICHOLSON

THE BABY

Small babe, tell me
      As you sat in your mother's cave
What did you build there,
      Little baby mine?

Sir, I made the tooth
      I invented the eye
I played out hair on a comb-harp
      I thought up the sigh.

I pounded the darkness to
      Guts, Heart and Head:
America, Eurasia and Africa
      I out of chaos led.

I fought the goblins
      For the heart;
'Twas a jewel they desired.
      But I held it.

I fought off the rats
      From the guts
They nibbled but I
      Smashed the mutts.

I choked the bat so intent
      For the diamond of my mind;
I caught him in the ogre's cellar
      The tub of blood behind.

And the darkness gave me
      Two boneless wands or swords;
I knew not their meaning then
      Whether traps or rewards.

One was the vorpal phallus
    Filled with jostling army.
Henhouse and palace
    Street crowds and history.

Two was the magic tongue
    Stuffed with names and numbers,
The string of song
    The waker from fallen slumbers.

My mother opened her grave
    I sprang out a giant
Into another cave
    Where I was a seed again,

Helpless and wriggly small
    As in my father's groin;
My Shakespeare's tongue a wawl
    And impotent my loin.

The sun-egg I must reach
    Was steeples far away,
The world that I must name
    Was shapeless, sneaky gray.

Is it wonder then I rage
    An old man one hour old,
A bridegroom come to a bride
    Careless unready and cold.

My wedding cake's still in the field:
    My bride is ninety and maggoty:
My groomsmen glaring hangmen:
    My bridal bed bouldery.

Small babe, tell me
    As you sit in your mother's cave
What do you build there.
    Little baby mine?

JAMES REANEY
From "A Sequence in Four Keys"

JESSIE MITCHELL'S MOTHER

Into her mother's bedroom to wash the ballooning body.
"My mother is jelly-hearted and she has a brain of jelly:
Sweet, quiver-soft, irrelevant. Not essential.
Only a habit would cry if she should die.
A pleasant sort of fool without the least iron. . . .
Are you better, mother, do you think it will come today?"
The stretched yellow rag that was Jessie Mitchell's mother
Reviewed her. Young, and so thin, and so straight.
So straight! as if nothing could ever bend her.
But poor men would bend her, and doing things with poor
    men,
Being much in bed, and babies would bend her over,
And the rest of things in life that were for poor women,
Coming to them grinning and pretty with intent to bend
    and to kill.
Comparisons shattered her heart, ate at her bulwarks:
The shabby and the bright: she, almost hating her
    daughter,
Crept into an old sly refuge: "Jessie's black
And her way will be black, and jerkier even than mine.
Mine, in fact, because I was lovely, had flowers
Tucked in the jerks, flowers were here and there. . . ."

117

She revived for the moment settled and dried-up triumphs,
Forced perfume into old petals, pulled up the droop,
Refueled
Triumphant long-exhaled breaths.
Her exquisite yellow youth. . . .

GWENDOLYN BROOKS

IN CHILDBED

In the middle of the night
Mother's spirit came and spoke to me,
    Looking weariful and white—
As 'twere untimely news she broke to me.

"O my daughter, joyed are you
To own the weetless child you mother there;
    'Men may search the wide world through,'
You think, 'nor find so fair another there!'

"Dear, this midnight time unwombs
Thousands just as rare and beautiful;
    Thousands whom High Heaven foredooms
To be as bright, as good, as dutiful.

"Source of ecstatic hopes and fears
And innocent maternal vanity,
    Your fond exploit but shapes for tears
New thoroughfares in sad humanity.

"Yet as you dream, so dreamt I
When Life stretched forth its morning ray to me;
Other views for by and by!". . . .
Such strange things did mother say to me.

THOMAS HARDY

TO AN UNBORN PAUPER CHILD

I

Breathe not, hid Heart: cease silently,
And though thy birth-hour beckons thee,
Sleep the long sleep:
The Doomsters heap
Travails and teens around us here,
And Time-wraiths turn our songsingings to fear.

II

Hark, how the peoples surge and sigh,
And laughters fail, and greetings die:
Hopes dwindle; yea,
Faiths waste away,
Affections and enthusiasms numb;
Thou canst not mend these things if thou dost come.

III

Had I the ear of wombèd souls
Ere their terrestrial chart unrolls,
And thou wert free
To cease, or be,
Then would I tell thee all I know,
And put it to thee: Wilt thou take Life so?

IV

Vain vow! No hint of mine may hence
To theeward fly: to thy locked sense
    Explain none can
    Life's pending plan:
Thou wilt thy ignorant entry make
Though skies spout fire and blood and nations quake.

V

Fain would I, dear, find some shut plot
Of earth's wide wold for thee, where not
    One tear, one qualm,
    Should break the calm.
But I am weak as thou and bare;
No man can change the common lot to rare.

VI

Must come and bide. And such are we—
Unreasoning, sanguine, visionary—
    That I can hope
    Health, love, friends, scope
In full for thee; can dream thou'lt find
Joys seldom yet attained by humankind!

THOMAS HARDY

PRAYER BEFORE BIRTH

I am not yet born; O hear me.
Let not the bloodsucking bat or the rat or the stoat or the
   clubfooted ghoul come near me.

I am not yet born, console me.
I fear that the human race may with tall walls wall me,
   with strong drugs dope me, with wise lies lure me,
      on black racks rack me, in blood-baths roll me.

I am not yet born; provide me
With water to dandle me, grass to grow for me, trees to
   talk to me, sky to sing to me, birds and a white light
      in the back of my mind to guide me.

I am not yet born; forgive me
For the sins that in me the world shall commit, my words
   When they speak me, my thoughts when they think me,
      my treason engendered by traitors beyond me,
         my life when they murder by means of my
            hands, my death when they live me.

I am not yet born; rehearse me
In the parts I must play and the cues I must take when
   old men lecture me, bureaucrats hector me, mountains
      frown at me, lovers laugh at me, the white
         waves call me to folly and the desert calls
           me to doom and the beggar refuses
              my gift and my children curse me.

I am not yet born; O hear me,
Let not the man who is beast or who thinks he is God
   come near me.

I am not yet born: O fill me
With strength against those who would freeze my
   humanity, would dragoon me into a lethal automaton,
      would make me a cog in a machine, a thing with
         one face, a thing, and against all those
           who would dissipate my entirety, would
             blow me like thistledown hither and
               thither or hither and thither
                 like water held in the
                   hands would spill me.

Let them not make me a stone and let them not spill me.
Otherwise kill me.

LOUIS MACNEICE

YOU'RE

   Clownlike, happiest on your hands,
   Feet to the stars, and moon-skulled,
   Gilled like a fish. A common-sense
   Thumbs-down on the dodo's mode.
   Wrapped up in yourself like a spool,
   Trawling your dark as owls do.
   Mute as a turnip from the Fourth
   Of July to All Fools' Day,
   O high-riser, my little loaf.

Vague as fog and looked for like mail.
Farther off than Australia.
Bent-backed Atlas, our traveled prawn.
Snug as a bud and at home
Like a sprat in a pickle jug
A creel of eels, all ripples.
Jumpy as a Mexican bean.
Right, like a well-done sum.
A clean slate, with your own face on.

SYLVIA PLATH

FOETAL SONG

The vehicle gives a lurch but seems
to know its destination.
In here, antique darkness. I guess at things.
Tremors of muscles communicate
secrets to me. I am nourished.
A surge of blood pounding sweet
blossoms my gentle head.
I am perfumed wax melted of holy candles
I am ready to be fingered and shaped.

This cave unfolds to my nudge, which
seems gentle but is hard as steel.
Coils of infinite steel are my secret.
Within this shadowless cave I am not confused
I think I am a fish, or a small seal.
I have an impulse to swim, but without
moving; *she* moves and I drift after. . . .
I am a trout silent and gilled, a tiny seal
a slippery monster knowing all secrets.
Where is she off to now?—in high heels.
I don't like the jiggle of high heels.
On the street we hear horns, drills, feel sleeves,
feel rushes of language moving by
and every stranger has possibly
my father's face.

Now we are in bed.
Her heart breathes quiet and I drink blood.
I am juicy and sweet and coiled.
Her dreams creep upon me through nightmare slots of
    windows
I cringe from them, unready.
I don't like such pictures.
Morning . . . and the safety of the day brings us
bedroom slippers, good.
Day at home, comfort in this sac,
three months from my birthday I dream
upon songs and eerie music, angels' flutes
that tear so stern upon earthly anger
(now they are arguing again).
Jokes and unjokes, married couple,
they clutch each other in water
I feel him nudge me but it is by accident.
The darkness of their sacs must be slimy with dead tides
and hide what they knew of ponds and knotty ropes of
    lilies.

It forsakes them now, cast into the same bed.
The tide throws them relentlessly into the same bed.
While he speaks to her I suck marrow from her bones.
It has a grainy white taste, a little salty.
Oxygen from her tremendous lungs tastes white too
but airy bubbly, it makes me dizzy . . .!

She speaks to him and her words do not matter.
Marrow and oxygen matter eternally. They are mine.
Sometimes she walks on concrete, my vehicle,
sometimes on gravel, on grass, on the
blank worn tides of our floors at home.
She and he, months ago, decided not to kill me.
I rise and fall now like seaweed fleshed to fish, a surprise.
I am grateful.
I am waiting for my turn.

JOYCE CAROL OATES

ON A LINE IN SANDBURG

"Where did the blood come from?
Before I bit, before I sucked
The red meat, the blood was there
Nourishing sweetly the roots of hair."

"The blood came from your mother
By way of the long gut-cord;
You were the pain in her side;
You were born on a blood-dark tide."

"My mother also was young
Once, but her cheeks were red
Even then. From its hidden source
The hot blood ran on its old course.

Where did the blood come from?"

R. S. THOMAS

GIVE ME MY INFANT NOW

Te-whaka-io-roa

Where are the hands and feet
That Tiki made? Gone with the gods.
Yes, O my children's mother!
Speak, and let me know
That I shall soon an infant see,
And priests shall stand before
The Ahu-rewa altar, where,
With incantations, they shall chant
To bones of those of ancient days,
And taunt the earthquake god.
Yes, yes, my children's mother,
Give me my infant now,
That, dandling it upon my knees,
My joy may be complete—
That I no more may feel
A want and ache not yet appeased.

ANON
From the Maori (trans. unknown)

Casualties

"THOU GOD OF THIS GREAT VAST, REBUKE THESE SURGES"

Enter PERICLES, *on shipboard.*

Per. Thou God of this great vast, rebuke these surges,
    Which wash both heaven and hell; and thou that hast
    Upon the winds command, bind them in brass,
    Having call'd them from the deep! O, still
    Thy deaf'ning, dreadful thunders; gently quench
    Thy nimble sulphurous flashes! O, how, Lychorida,
    How does my queen? Thou stormest venomously;
    Wilt thou spit all thyself? The seaman's whistle
    Is as a whisper in the ears of death,
    Unheard. Lychorida!—Lucina, O
    Divinest patroness, and midwife gentle
    To those that cry by night, convey thy deity
    Aboard our dancing boat; make swift the pangs
    Of my queen's travails! Now, Lychorida!

Enter LYCHORIDA, *with an infant.*

Lyc. Here is a thing too young for such a place,
    Who, if it had conceit, would die, as I
    Am like to do. Take in your arms this piece
    Of your dead queen.
Per.   How? how, Lychorida?
Lyc. Patience, good sir; do not assist the storm.
    Here's all that is left living of your queen,
    A little daughter: for the sake of it,
    Be manly, and take comfort.
Per.   O you gods!
    Why do you make us love your goodly gifts,
    And snatch them straight away? We here below
    Recall not what we give, and therein may
    Use honour with you.
Lyc.   Patience, good sir,
    even for this charge.

Per. Now, mild may be thy life!
　　For a more blusterous birth had never babe;
　　Quiet and gentle thy conditions! for
　　Thou art the rudeliest welcome to this world
　　That e'er was prince's child. Happy what follows!
　　Thou hast as chiding a nativity
　　As fire, air, water, earth, and heaven can make,
　　To herald thee from the womb. Poor inch of nature!
　　Even at the first thy loss is more than can
　　Thy portage quit, with all thou canst find here.
　　Now the good gods throw their best eyes upon't!

WILLIAM SHAKESPEARE

From *Pericles, Prince of Tyre*, Act 3, Scene 1

CHICAGO BOY BABY

The baby picked from an ash barrel by the night police
came to the hospital of the Franciscan brothers
in a diaper and a white sheet.

It was a windy night in October, leaves and geese
　　scurrying
across the north sky, and the curb pigeons more ravenous
than ever for city corn in the cracks of the street stones.

The two policemen who picked the baby from the ash
　　barrel
are grayheads; they talk about going on the pension list
soon; they talk about whether the baby, surely a big man
now, votes this year for Smith or Hoover.

CARL SANDBURG

A COLD FRONT

This woman with a dead face
has seven foster children
and a new baby of her own in
spite of that. She wants pills

for an abortion and says,
Uh hum, in reply to me while
her blanketed infant makes
unrelated grunts of salutation.

She looks at me with her mouth
open and blinks her expressionless
carved eyes, like a cat
on a limb too tired to go higher

from its tormentors. And still
the baby chortles in its spit
and there is a dull flush
almost of beauty to the woman's face

as she says, looking at me
quietly, I won't have any more.
In a case like this I know
quick action is the main thing.

WILLIAM CARLOS WILLIAMS

"CORINNA, HAVING TRIED, WITH HER OWN HAND"

Corinna, having tried, with her own hand,
To cure herself of pregnancy, lies low.
I should be angry at the deed she planned,
The risk she took, and never let me know.
But anger yields to fear—I was the cause,
At least, I might have been; the chance was there.
Since *posse* may be *esse*, if I was,
O Isis, bring us comfort, hear my prayer!

Come from Canopus, Pharos rich in palms,
Where seven-mouthed Nile moves gliding to the sea,
Osiris speed you here, with healing balms,
Give life to her, and so give life to me.
She never failed your services beside
Those laurels where the Gallic horsemen ride.

And you, Birth-Goddess, pitying the dole
Of women in long labour, great with child,
Hear the entreaties of an anguished soul,
Have pity on her, merciful and mild!
Favour my prayers, and intercede for her—
She is not all unworthy of your grace—
And I, white-robed, will be your minister,
Bring you due fits, in proper time and place.

And more than that—by my own hand engraved
A verse upon a votive stone will read
"Ovid is grateful for Corinna saved,"
Memorial in word as well as need.
Frightened, and tactless, like so many men,
I add, "Corinna, don't do this again!"

OVID

From *Amores* II, 13 (trans. Rolfe Humphries)

"WHEN LIL'S HUSBAND GOT
DEMOBBED, I SAID—"

When Lil's husband got demobbed. I said—
I didn't mince my words, I said to her myself,
HURRY UP PLEASE ITS TIME
Now Albert's coming back, make yourself a bit smart.
He'll want to know what you done with that money he
  gave you
To get yourself some teeth. He did, I was there.
You have them all out, Lil, and get a nice set,
He said, I swear, I can't bear to look at you.
And no more can't I, I said, and think of poor Albert,
He's been in the army four years, he wants a good time,
And if you don't give it him, there's others will, I said.
Oh is there, she said. Something o' that, I said.
Then I'll know who to thank, she said, and give me a
  straight look.
HURRY UP PLEASE ITS TIME
If you don't like it you can get on with it, I said.
Others can pick and choose if you can't.
But if Albert makes off, it won't be for lack of telling.

You ought to be ashamed, I said, to look so antique.
(And her only thirty-one.)
I can't help it, she said, pulling a long face,
It's them pills I took, to bring it off, she said.
(She's had five already, and nearly died of young George.)
The chemist said it would be all right, but I've never been
    the same.
You *are* a proper fool, I said.
Well, if Albert won't leave you alone, there it is, I said,
What you get married for if you don't want children?
HURRY UP PLEASE ITS TIME
Well, that Sunday Albert was home, they had a hot
    gammon,
And they asked me in to dinner, to get the beauty of it
    hot—
HURRY UP PLEASE ITS TIME
HURRY UP PLEASE ITS TIME
Goonight Bill. Goonight Lou. Goonight May, Goonight.
Ta ta. Goonight. Goonight.
Good night, ladies, good night, sweet ladies, good night,
    good night.

T. S. ELIOT
From *The Waste Land*

RAVENS

As we came through the gate to look at the few new
    lambs
On the skyline of lawn smoothness,
A raven bundled itself into air from midfield
And slid away under hard glistenings, low and guilty.
Sheep nibbling, kneeling to nibble the reluctant nibbled
    grass.
Sheep staring, their jaws pausing to think, then chewing
    again,
Then pausing. Over there a new lamb
Just getting up, bumping its mother's nose
As she nibbles the sugar coating off it
While the tattered banners of her triumph swing and drip
    from her rear-end.
She sneezes and a glim of water flashes from her rear-end.
She sneezes again and again, till she's emptied.
She carries on investigating her new present and seeing
    how it works.
Over here is something else. But you are still interested
In that new one, and its new spark of voice,
And its tininess.
Now over here, where the raven was,
Is what interests you next. Born dead,
Twisted like a scarf, a lamb of an hour or two,
Its insides, the various jellies and crimsons and
    transparencies
And threads and tissues pulled out
In straight lines, like tent ropes
From its upward belly opened like a lamb-wool slipper,
The fine anatomy of silvery ribs on display and the cavity,
The head also emptied through the eye-sockets,
The woolly limbs swathed in birth-yolk and impossible
To tell now which in all this field of quietly nibbling
    sheep

Was its mother. I explain
That it died being born. We should have been here, to
  help it.
So it died being born. "And did it cry?" you cry.
I pick up the dangling greasy weight by the hooves soft as
  dogs' pads
That had trodden only womb-water
And its raven-drawn strings dangle and trail,
Its loose head joggles, and "Did it cry?" you cry again.
Its two-fingered feet splay in their skin between the
  pressures
Of my finger and thumb. And there is another,
Just born, all black, splaying its tripod, inching its new
  points
Towards its mother, and testing the note
It finds in its mouth. But you have eyes now
Only for the tattered bundle of throwaway lamb.
"Did it cry?" you keep asking, in a three-year-old
  field-wide
Piercing persistence. "Oh yes" I say "it cried."

Though this one was lucky insofar
As it made the attempt into a warm wind
And its first day of death was blue and warm
The magpies gone quiet with domestic happiness
And skylarks not worrying about anything
And the blackthorn budding confidently
And the skyline of hills, after millions of hard years,
Sitting soft.

TED HUGHES

"SO WHEN THE HAMMERS OF THE WITNESSES OF HEAVEN ARE RAISED ALL TOGETHER"

I

So when the hammers of the witnesses of heaven are
                                        raised all together
up yonder

there will be dumbness in the choir tonight

when the voices are raised all together
black kites flying on what should be a holiday

there will be silence in the cathedral

a woman loves a man

she will lick the sweat from his forehead
she will walk miles to see him
and wait for him by the corner

she will bear his children loudly

upon the earth is firm foot
toes searching the top-soil
gripping

the instep, the angles of knub, heel and ankle
are grey with the roads
with the long hypodermics of noon

the dress tucks itself over the black buttocks
into the suction of thighs
the hip is a scythe
grass growling along the hillside

she will bend forward with the hoe: *huh*
and the gravel will answer her: *so*
she will swing upward with the hoe: *huh*
and the bones of the plantation will come ringing to meet
    her: *so*
her sweat will water the onions and the shaddock and the
    wild thyme

she will bear his children proudly

but when he turns sour on her
scowling, wiping her face with his anger
stiffening his spine beside her on the bed
not caressing her curves with eye-

lash or word or jook of the elbow
she will curdle like milk
the bones of the plantation will come ringing to meet her:
    so

the bucket will rattle in the morning at the stan'pipe

but there will be no water
the skillet will rattle at midday
but there will be no milk
she will become the mother of bastards

* * * *

III

if there are ways of saying yes
i do not know them

if there are dreams
i cannot recall them to the light

if there is rage
it is cool cinder

in the heat of the day
i swear i will sweat no more

knife, bill-hook, sweet bramble
i will burn in my bush of screams

hoe: i will work
    root, mud, marl, burden

needle: i will sew
    thread, stitch, embroidered image

jesus: i will serve thee
    knee, copper, rain falling from heaviest heaven of
                                   storm

but i will drink you no more
torch you no more
sweaten you out on the lumps of the mattress no longer

the hoe will stand in the corner by the back door
cane flowers will flicker with rainflies
but there will be no crop-over songs

the fields will grow green soundlessly
the roots will fatten until they burst
and then they will fatten again until they burst

but there will be no kukoo or okro or jug

the needle will grow rusty in the cloth:
pin, pinch of thread, thimble:
it will make no silver track and tremble far into the night

no dress will take shape over my head
slipping down like water over my naked breasts

the seats of the chapel will remain empty
the wicks burning at altar till daybreak
fattened by shadows and moths

your foetus i will poison
dark dark mollusc
spinach, susum, suck-de-well-dry bush

the child still fish, still lizard,
wrinkled gill and croaking gizzard

i will destroy: blinding the eyeballs
pulling out the flag of its tongue by the shreds
ripping open the egg of its skull with sunless manchioneal
blisters

i will carry the wet twitching rag
bearing your face, conveying your futureless race
in its burst bag of balls to your doorstep

maaaa: it will cry
and the windows will be pulled down tight against the
wind

meeowww: it will howl
and a black dog will go prowling past the dripping pit
latrines

and when the moon is a wild
flower falling through cloud, from patch to shade you will
see it

once our child, our toil of touch, our sharing
sitting under the sandbox tree, smiling smiling

slipping its plate of bleed

IV

these images of love i leave you
when i no longer need you

man, manwart, manimal

EDWARD KAMAU BRATHWAITE
From "Cherries"

Prophetic and Philosophical

"SICILIAN MUSE, I WOULD TRY NOW
A SOMEWHAT GRANDER THEME"

Sicilian Muse, I would try now a somewhat grander
theme.
Shrubberies or meek tamarisks are not for all: but if it's
Forests I sing, may the forests be worthy of a consul.
Ours is the crowning era foretold in prophecy:
Born of Time, a great new cycle of centuries
Begins. Justice returns to earth, the Golden Age
Returns, and its first-born comes down from heaven above.
Look kindly, chaste Lucina, upon this infant's birth,
For with him shall hearts of iron cease, and hearts of gold
Inherit the whole earth—yes, Apollo reigns now.
And it's while you are consul—you, Pollio—that this
glorious
Age shall dawn, the march of its great months begin.
You at our head, mankind shall be freed from its age-long
fear,
All stains of our past wickedness being cleansed away.
This child shall enter into the life of the gods, behold
them
Walking with antique heroes, and himself be seen of
them,
And rule a world made peaceful by his father's virtuous
acts.
Child, your first birthday presents will come from
nature's wild—
Small presents: earth will shower you with romping ivy,
foxgloves,
Bouquets of gipsy lilies and sweetly-smiling acanthus.
Goats shall walk home, their udders taut with milk, and
nobody
Herding them: the ox will have no fear of the lion:
Silk-soft blossom will grow from your very cradle to lap
you.

But snakes will die, and so will fair-seeming, poisonous
                                                    plants.
Everywhere the commons will breathe of spice and
                                                incense.
    But when you are old enough to read about famous men
And your father's deeds, to comprehend what manhood
                                                    means,
Then a slow flush of tender gold shall mantle the great
                                                    plains,
Then shall grapes hang wild and reddening on thorn-trees,
And honey sweat like dew from the hard bark of oaks.
Yet there'll be lingering traces still of our primal error,
Prompting us to dare the seas in ships, to girdle
Our cities round with walls and break the soil with
                                            ploughshares.
A second Argo will carry her crew of chosen heroes,
A second Tiphys steer her. And wars—yes, even wars
There'll be; and great Achilles must sail for Troy again.
    Later, when the years have confirmed you in full
                                                manhood,
Traders will retire from the sea, from the pine-built vessels
They used for commerce: every land will be self-
                                            supporting.
The soil will need no harrowing, the vine no pruning-
                                                knife;
And the tough ploughman may at last unyoke his oxen.
We shall stop treating wool with artificial dyes,
For the ram himself in his pasture will change his fleece's
                                                colour,
Now to a charming purple, now to a saffron hue,
And grazing lambs will dress themselves in coats of scarlet.
    "Run, looms, and weave this future!"—thus have the
                                            Fates spoken,
In unison with the unshakeable intent of Destiny.
    Come soon, dear child of the gods, Jupiter's great
                                                viceroy!

Come soon—the time is near—to begin your life
                                          illustrious!
Look how the round and ponderous globe bows to salute
                                                    you,
The lands, the stretching leagues of sea, the unplumbed
                                                     sky!
Look how the whole creation exults in the age to come!
  If but the closing days of a long life were prolonged
For me, and I with breath enough to tell your story,
Oh then I should not be worsted at singing by Thracian
                                                 Orpheus
Or Linus—even though Linus were backed by Calliope
His mother, and Orpheus by his father, beauteous Apollo.
Should Pan compete with me, and Arcady judge us, even
Pan, great Pan, with Arcadian judges, would lose the
                                               contest.
  Begin, dear babe, and smile at your mother to show you
                                            know her—
This is the tenth month now, and she is sick of waiting.
Begin, dear babe. The boy who does not smile at his
                                               mother
Will never deserve to sup with a god or sleep with a
goddess.

                                            VIRGIL
                      Eclogue 4 (trans. C. Day Lewis)

147

"THIS ROYAL INFANT"

Enter Trumpets sounding: then two Aldermen, LORD
MAYOR, GARTER, CRANMER, DUKE OF NORFOLK
with his marshal's staff, DUKE OF SUFFOLK, *two noblemen
bearing great standing bowls for the christening gifts: then
four noblemen bearing a canopy, under which the* DUCH-
ESS OF NORFOLK, *godmother, bearing the child richly
habited in a mantle, etc.; train borne by a lady: then follows
the* MARCHIONESS DORSET, *the other godmother, and
ladies. The troop pass once about the stage, and* GARTER
SPEAKS.

Gart. Heaven, from thy endless goodness, send prosperous
life, long and ever happy, to the high and mighty princess of
England, Elizabeth.

Flourish. Enter KING *and Guard.*

Cran. (Kneeling.) And to your royal grace, and the good
      queen,
    My noble partners and myself thus pray,
    All comfort, joy in this most gracious lady,
    Heaven ever laid up to make parents happy,
    May hourly fall upon ye.
King   Thank you good lord archbishop:
    What is her name?
Cran.   Elizabeth.
King   Stand up lord;
             (The king kisses the child.)
    With this kiss take my blessing: God protect thee,
    Into whose hand I give thy life.
Cran.   Amen.
King My noble gossips, y'have been too prodigal;
    I thank ye heartily: so shall this lady,
    When she has so much English.

Cran.   Let me speak sir,
For heaven now bids me; and the words I utter,
Let none think flattery, for they'll find 'em truth.
This royal infant (heavens still move about her)
Though in her cradle, yet now promises
Upon this land a thousand thousand blessings,
Which time shall bring to ripeness: she shall be
(But few now living can behold that goodness)
A pattern to all princes living with her,
And all that shall succeed: Saba was never
More covetous of wisdom and fair virtue
Than this pure soul shall be. All princely graces
That mould up such a mighty piece as this is,
With all the virtues that attend the good,
Shall still be doubled on her. Truth shall nurse her,
Holy and heavenly thoughts still counsel her;
She shall be lov'd and fear'd: her own shall bless her;
Her foes shake like a field of beaten corn,
And hang their heads with sorrow: good grows with her;
In her days every man shall eat in safety
Under his own vine what he plants, and sing
The merry songs of peace to all his neighbours.
God shall be truly known, and those about her
From her shall read the perfect ways of honour,
And by those claim their greatness, not by blood.
Nor shall this peace sleep with her; but, as when
The bird of wonder dies, the maiden phoenix,
Her ashes new create another heir
As great in admiration as herself,
So shall she leave her blessedness to one
(When heaven shall call her from this cloud of
    darkness)
Who from the sacred ashes of her honour
Shall star-like rise, as great in fame as she was,
And so stand fix'd. Peace, plenty, love, truth, terror,
That were the servants to this chosen infant,

Shall then be his, and like a vine grow to him;
Wherever the bright sun of heaven shall shine,
His honour and the greatness of his name
Shall be, and make new nations. He shall flourish,
And like a mountain cedar, reach his branches
To all the plains about him: our children's children
Shall see this, and bless heaven.

King   Thou speakest wonders.

Cran. She shall be, to the happiness of England,
An aged princess; many days shall see her,
And yet no day without a deed to crown it.
Would I had known no more; but she must die,
She must, the saints must have her; yet a virgin,
A most unspotted lily shall she pass
To th'ground, and all the world shall mourn her.

King O lord archbishop,
Thou hast made me now a man; never before
This happy child did I get anything.
This oracle of comfort has so pleas'd me,
That when I am in heaven I shall desire
To see what this child does, and praise my maker.
I thank ye all. To you my good lord mayor,
And your good brethren, I am much beholding:
I have receiv'd much honour by your presence,
And ye shall find me thankful. Lead the way lords,
Ye must all see the queen, and she must thank ye,
She will be sick else. This day, no man think
He has business at his house; for all shall stay:
This little one shall make it Holy-day.   *Exeunt.*

WILLIAM SHAKESPEARE
From *Henry VIII*, Act 5, Scene 4

ON THE MORNING OF CHRIST'S NATIVITY

I

This is the month, and this the happy morn,
Wherein the Son of Heaven's Eternal King,
Of wedded maid and virgin mother born,
Our great redemption from above did bring;
For so the holy sages once did sing,
   That he our deadly forfeit should release,
And with his Father work us a perpetual peace.

II

That glorious form, that light unsufferable,
And that far-beaming blaze of majesty,
Wherewith he wont at Heaven's high council-table
To sit the midst of Trinal Unity,
He laid aside, and, here with us to be,
   Forsook the courts of everlasting day,
And chose with us a darksome house of mortal clay.

III

Say, Heavenly Muse, shall not thy sacred vein
Afford a present to the Infant God?
Hast thou no verse, no hymn, or solemn strain,
To welcome him to this his new abode,
Now while the heaven, by the Sun's team untrod,
   Hath took no print of the approaching light,
And all the spangled host keep watch in squadrons bright?

IV

See how from far upon the eastern road
The star-led wizards haste with odours sweet!
Oh! run; prevent them with thy humble ode,
And lay it lowly at his blessed feet;
Have thou the honour first thy Lord to greet,
　And join thy voice unto the Angel Quire,
From out his secret altar touched with hallowed fire.

THE HYMN

I

It was the winter wild,
　While the heaven-born child
All meanly wrapt in the rude manger lies;
　Nature, in awe to him,
　Had doffed her gaudy trim,
With her great Master so to sympathise:
It was no season then for her
To wanton with the Sun, her lusty paramour.

II

Only with speeches fair
　She woos the gentle air
To hide her guilty front with innocent snow,
　And on her naked shame,
　Pollute with sinful blame,
The saintly veil of maiden white to throw;
Confounded, that her Maker's eyes
Should look so near upon her foul deformities.

III

But he, her fears to cease,
Sent down the meek-eyed Peace:
She, crowned with olive green, came softly sliding
Down through the turning sphere,
His ready harbinger,
With turtle wing the amorous clouds dividing;
And, waving wide her myrtle wand,
She strikes a universal peace through sea and land.

IV

No war, or battle's sound,
Was heard the world around;
The idle spear and shield were high uphung;
The hookèd chariot stood,
Unstained with hostile blood;
The trumpet spake not to the armèd throng;
And kings sat still with awful eye,
As if they surely knew their sovran Lord was by.

V

But peaceful was the night
Wherein the Prince of Light
His reign of peace upon the earth began.
The winds, with wonder whist,
Smoothly the waters kissed,
Whispering new joys to the mild Oceán,
Who now hath quite forgot to rave,
While birds of calm sit brooding on the charmèd wave.

VI

    The stars, with deep amaze,
    Stand fixed in steadfast gaze,
Bending one way their precious influence,
    And will not take their flight,
    For all the morning light,
Or Lucifer that often warned them thence;
But in their glimmering orbs did glow,
Until their Lord himself bespake, and bid them go.

VII

    And, though the shady gloom
    Had given day her room,
The Sun himself withheld his wonted speed,
    And hid his head for shame,
    As his inferior flame
The new-enlightened world no more should need:
He saw a greater Sun appear
Than his bright throne or burning axletree could bear.

VIII

    The shepherds on the lawn,
    Or ere the point of dawn,
Sat simply chatting in a rustic row;
    Full little thought they than
    That the mighty Pan
Was kindly come to live with them below:
Perhaps their loves, or else their sheep,
Was all that did their silly thoughts so busy keep.

IX

When such music sweet
  Their hearts and ears did greet
As never was by mortal finger strook,
  Divinely-warbled voice
  Answering the stringed noise,
As all their souls in blissful rapture took:
The air, such pleasure loth to lose,
With thousand echoes still prolongs each heavenly close.

X

Nature, that heard such sound
  Beneath the hollow round
Of Cynthia's seat the Airy region thrilling,
  Now was almost won
  To think her part was done,
And that her reign had here its last fulfilling:
She knew such harmony alone
Could hold all Heaven and Earth in happier union.

XI

At last surrounds their sight
  A globe of circular light,
That with long beams the shamefaced Night arrayed;
  The helmèd cherubim
  And sworded seraphim
Are seen in glittering ranks with wings displayed,
Harping in loud and solemn quire,
With unexpressive notes, to Heaven's new-born Heir.

XII

Such music (as 'tis said)
   Before was never made,
But when of old the Sons of Morning sung,
   While the Creator great
   His constellations set,
And the well balanced World on hinges hung,
And cast the dark foundations deep,
And bid the weltering waves their oozy channel keep.

XIII

Ring out, ye crystal spheres!
   Once bless our human ears,
If ye have power to touch our senses so;
   And let your silver chime
   Move in melodious time;
And let the bass of heaven's deep organ blow;
And with your ninefold harmony
Make up full consort to the angelic symphony.

XIV

For, if such holy song
   Enwrap our fancy long,
Time will run back and fetch the Age of Gold;
   And speckled Vanity
   Will sicken soon and die;
And leprous Sin will melt from earthly mould;
And Hell itself will pass away,
And leave her dolorous mansions to the peering day.

XV

Yea, Truth and Justice then
   Will down return to men,
Orbed in a rainbow; and, like glories wearing,
   Mercy will sit between,
   Throned in celestial sheen,
With radiant feet the tissued clouds down steering;
And Heaven, as at some festival,
Will open wide the gates of her high palace-hall.

XVI

But wisest Fate says No,
   This must not yet be so;
The Babe yet lies in smiling infancy
   That on the bitter cross
   Must redeem our loss,
So both himself and us to glorify:
Yet first, to those ychained in sleep,
The wakeful trump of doom must thunder through the
   deep,

XVII

With such a horrid clang
   As on Mount Sinai rang,
While the red fire and smouldering clouds outbrake:
   The aged Earth, agast,
   With terror of that blast,
Shall from the surface to the centre shake,
When, at the world's last session,
The dreadful Judge in middle air shall spread his throne.

XVIII

And then at last our bliss
    Full and perfect is,
But now begins; for from this happy day
    The Old Dragon under ground,
    In straiter limits bound,
Not half so far casts his usurpèd sway,
And, wroth to see his kingdom fail,
Swinges the scaly horror of his folded tail.

XIX

The Oracles are dumb;
    No voice or hideous hum
Runs through the archèd roof in words deceiving.
    Apollo from his shrine
    Can no more divine,
With hollow shriek the steep of Delphos leaving.
No nightly trance, or breathèd spell,
Inspires the pale-eyed priest from the prophetic cell.

XX

The lonely mountains o'er,
    And the resounding shore,
A voice of weeping heard and loud lament;
    From haunted spring, and dale
    Edged with poplar pale,
The parting Genius is with sighing sent;
With flower-inwoven tresses torn
The Nymphs in twilight shade of tangled thickets mourn.

XXI

In consecrated earth,
And on the holy hearth,
The Lars and Lemures moan with midnight plaint;
In urns, and altars round,
A drear and dying sound
Affrights the flamens at their service quaint;
And the chill marble seems to sweat,
While each peculiar Power forgoes his wonted seat.

XXII

Peor and Baälim
Forsake their temples dim,
With that twice-battered God of Palestine;
And moonèd Ashtaroth,
Heaven's queen and mother both,
Now sits not girt with tapers' holy shine:
The Libyc Hammon shrinks his horn;
In vain the Tyrian maids their wounded Thammuz
mourn.

XXIII

And sullen Moloch, fled,
Hath left in shadows dread
His burning idol all of blackest hue;
In vain with cymbal's ring
They call the grisly king,
In dismal dance about the furnace blue;
The brutish gods of Nile as fast,
Isis, and Orus, and the dog Anubis, haste.

XXIV

Nor is Osiris seen
  In Memphian grove or green,
Trampling the unshowered grass with lowings loud;
  Nor can he be at rest
  Within his sacred chest;
Nought but profoundest Hell can be his shroud;
In vain, with timbrelled anthems dark,
The sable-stolèd sorcerers bear his worshipped ark.

XXV

He feels from Juda's land
  The dreaded Infant's hand;
The rays of Bethlehem blind his dusky eyn;
  Nor all the gods beside
  Longer dare abide,
Not Typhon huge ending in snaky twine:
Our Babe, to show his Godhead true,
Can in his swaddling bands control the damnèd crew.

XXVI

So, when the sun in bed,
  Curtained with cloudy red,
Pillows his chin upon an orient wave,
  The flocking shadows pale
  Troop to the infernal jail,
Each fettered ghost slips to his several grave,
And the yellow-skirted fays
Fly after the night-steeds, leaving their moon-loved maze.

XXVII

But see! the Virgin blest
Hath laid her Babe to rest.
Time is our tedious song should here have ending:
Heaven's youngest-teemèd star
Hath fixed her polished car,
Her sleeping Lord with handmaid lamp attending;
And all about the courtly stable
Bright-harnessed Angels sit in order serviceable.

JOHN MILTON

"PARTS OF THE WHOLE ARE WE; BUT GOD THE WHOLE"

Parts of the Whole are we; but God the Whole;
Who gives us Life, and animating Soul.
For Nature cannot from a Part derive
That Being, which the Whole can only give:
He perfect, stable; but imperfect We,
Subject to Change, and diff'rent in Degree.
Plants, Beasts, and Man; and as our Organs are,
We more or less of his Perfection share.
But by a long Descent, th' Etherial Fire
Corrupts; and Forms, the mortal Part, expire:
As he withdraws his Vertue, so they pass,
And the same Matter makes another Mass:
This Law th' Omniscient Pow'r was pleas'd to give,
That ev'ry Kind should by Succession live;
That Individuals die, his Will ordains;
The propagated Species still remains.

The Monarch Oak, the Patriarch of the Trees,
Shoots rising up, and spreads by slow Degrees:
Three Centuries he grows, and three he stays,
Supreme in State; and in three more decays:
So wears the paving Pebble in the Street,
And Towns and Tow'rs their fatal Periods meet.
So Rivers, rapid once, now naked like,
Forsaken of their Springs; and leave their Channels dry.
So Man, at first a Drop, dilates with Heat,
Then form'd, the little Heart begins to beat;
Secret he feeds, unknowing in the Cell;
At length, for Hatching ripe, he breaks the Shell,
And struggles into Breath, and cries for Aid;
Then, helpless, in his Mother's Lap is laid.
He creeps, he walks, and issuing into Man,
Grudges their Life, from whence his own began.
Retchless of Laws, affects to rule alone,
Anxious to reign, and restless on the Throne:
First vegetive, then feels, and reasons last;
Rich of Three Souls, and lives all three to waste.
Some thus; but thousands more in Flow'r of Age:
For few arrive to run the latter Stage.
Sunk in the first, in Battel some are slain,
And others whelm'd beneath the stormy Main.
What makes all this, but *Jupiter* the King,
At whose Command we perish, and we spring?
Then 'tis our best, since thus ordain'd to die,
To make a Vertue of Necessity.

JOHN DRYDEN
From *Fables Ancient and Modern*,
"Palamon and Arcite", III

ODE
INTIMATIONS OF IMMORTALITY
FROM RECOLLECTIONS OF EARLY CHILDHOOD

The child is father of the man;
And I could wish my days to be
Bound each to each by natural piety.

There was a time when meadow, grove, and stream,
  The earth, and every common sight,
       To me did seem
      Apparelled in celestial light,
  The glory and the freshness of a dream.
It is not now as it hath been of yore;—
      Turn wheresoe'er I may,
      By night or day,
The things which I have seen I now can see no more.

      The Rainbow comes and goes,
      And lovely is the Rose,
      The Moon doth with delight
  Look round her when the heavens are bare,
      Waters on a starry night
      Are beautiful and fair;
  The sunshine is a glorious birth;
  But yet I know, where'er I go,
That there hath pass'd away a glory from the earth.

Now, while the birds thus sing a joyous song,
  And while the young lambs bound
      As to the tabor's sound,
To me alone there came a thought of grief:
A timely utterance gave that thought relief,
      And I again am strong:
The cataracts blow their trumpets from the steep;
No more shall grief of mine the season wrong;
I hear the Echoes through the mountains throng,
  The Winds come to me from the fields of sleep,
      And all the earth is gay;
        Land and sea
     Give themselves up to jollity,
      And with the heart of May
    Doth every Beast keep holiday;—
      Thou Child of Joy,
Shout round me, let me hear thy shouts, thou happy
  Shepherd-boy.

Ye blessèd creatures, I have heard the call
  Ye to each other make; I see
The heavens laugh with you in your jubilee;
  My heart is at your festival,
    My head hath its coronal,
The fulness of your bliss, I feel—I feel it all.
      Oh evil day! if I were sullen
      While Earth herself is adorning,
       This sweet May-morning,.
     And the Children are culling
      On every side,
    In a thousand valleys far and wide,
    Fresh flowers; while the sun shines warm,
And the Babe leaps up on his Mother's arm:—

I hear, I hear, with joy I hear!
—But there's a Tree, of many, one,
A single field which I have looked upon,
Both of them speak of something that is gone;
         The Pansy at my feet
         Doth the same tale repeat:
Whither is fled the visionary gleam?
Where is it now, the glory and the dream?

Our birth is but a sleep and a forgetting:
The Soul that rises with us, our life's Star,
         Hath had elsewhere its setting,
            And cometh from afar:
         Not in entire forgetfulness,
         And not in utter nakedness,
But trailing clouds of glory do we come
         From God, who is our home:
Heaven lies about us in our infancy!
Shades of the prison-house begin to close
         Upon the growing Boy,
But he beholds the light, and whence it flows,
         He sees it in his joy;
The Youth, who daily farther from the east
         Must travel, still is Nature's Priest,
         And by the vision splendid
         Is on his way attended;
At length the Man perceives it die away,
And fade into the light of common day.

Earth fills her lap with pleasures of her own;
Yearnings she hath in her own natural kind,
And, even with something of a Mother's mind,
  And no unworthy aim,
  The homely Nurse doth all she can
To make her Foster-child, her Inmate Man,
  Forget the glories he hath known,
And that imperial palace whence he came.

Behold the Child among his new-born blisses,
A six years' Darling of a pigmy size!
See, where 'mid work of his own hand he lies,
Fretted by sallies of his mother's kisses,
With light upon him from his father's eyes!
See, at his feet, some little plan or chart,
Some fragment from his dream of human life,
Shaped by himself with newly-learnèd art
  A wedding or a festival,
  A mourning or a funeral;
   And this hath now his heart,
   And unto this he frames his song:
    Then will he fit his tongue
To dialogues of business, love, or strife;
   But it will not be long
   Ere this be thrown aside,
   And with new joy and pride
The little Actor cons another part;
Filling from time to time his "humorous stage"
With all the Persons, down to palsied Age,
That Life brings with her in her equipage;
  As if his whole vocation
  Were endless imitation.

Thou, whose exterior semblance doth belie
   Thy Soul's immensity;
Thou best Philosopher, who yet dost keep
Thy heritage, thou Eye among the blind,
That, deaf and silent, read'st the eternal deep,
Haunted for ever by the eternal mind,—
   Mighty Prophet! Seer blest!
   On whom those truths do rest,
Which we are toiling all our lives to find,
In darkness lost, the darkness of the grave;
Thou, over whom thy Immortality
Broods like the Day, a Master o'er a Slave,
A Presence which is not to be put by;
Thou little Child, yet glorious in the might
Of heaven-born freedom on thy being's height,
Why with such earnest pains dost thou provoke
The years to bring the inevitable yoke,
Thus blindly with thy blessedness at strife?
Full soon thy Soul shall have her earthly freight,
And custom lie upon thee with a weight,
Heavy as frost, and deep almost as life!

   O joy! that in our embers
   Is something that doth live,
   That Nature yet remembers
   What was so fugitive!
The thought of our past years in me doth breed
Perpetual benediction: not indeed
For that which is most worthy to be blest;

Delight and liberty, the simple creed
Of Childhood, whether busy or at rest,
With new-fledged hope still fluttering in his breast:—
   Not for these I raise
    The song of thanks and praise;
  But for those obstinate questionings
   Of sense and outward things,
   Fallings from us, vanishings;
   Blank misgivings of a Creature
Moving about in worlds not realized,
High instincts before which our mortal Nature
Did tremble like a guilty thing surprised:
   But for those first affections,
   Those shadowy recollections,
    Which, be they what they may
Are yet the fountain-light of all our day,
Are yet a master-light of all our seeing;
   Uphold us, cherish, and have power to make
Our noisy years seem moments in the being
Of the eternal Silence: truths that wake,
    To perish never;
Which neither listlessness, nor mad endeavour,
    Nor Man nor Boy,
Nor all that is at enmity with joy,
Can utterly abolish or destroy!
   Hence in a season of calm weather
    Though inland far we be,
Our Souls have sight of that immortal sea
    Which brought us hither,
    Can in a moment travel thither,
And see the Children sport upon the shore,
And hear the mighty waters rolling evermore.

Then sing, ye Birds, sing, sing a joyous song!
          And let the young Lambs bound
          As to the tabor's sound!
We in thought will join your throng,
          Ye that pipe and ye that play,
          Ye that through your hearts today
          Feel the gladness of the May!
What though the radiance which was once so bright
Be now for ever taken from my sight,
          Though nothing can bring back the hour
Of splendour in the grass, of glory in the flower;
          We will grieve not, rather find
          Strength in what remains behind;
          In the primal sympathy
          Which having been must ever be;
          In the soothing thoughts that spring
          Out of human suffering;
          In the faith that looks through death,
In years that bring the philosophic mind.

And O, ye Fountains, Meadows, Hills, and Groves,
Forebode not any severing of our loves!
Yet in my heart of hearts I feel your might;
I only have relinquished one delight
To live beneath your more habitual sway.
I love the Brooks which down their channels fret,
Even more than when I tripped lightly as they;

The innocent brightness of a new-born Day
      Is lovely yet;
The Clouds that gather round the setting sun
Do take a sober colouring from an eye
That hath kept watch o'er man's mortality;
Another race hath been, and other palms are won.
Thanks to the human heart by which we live,
Thanks to its tenderness, its joys, and fears,
To me the meanest flower that blows can give
Thoughts that do often lie too deep for tears.

WILLIAM WORDSWORTH

Christmas: the Birth

First
Shepherd

Hail, comly and clene,
　Hail, yong child!
Hail, maker, as I meene,
　Of a maden so milde!
Thou has warèd, I weene,
　The warlo so wilde;
The fals giler of teen,
　Now goes he begilde.
　　　Lo! he merys,
Lo! he laghes, my sweting.
A welfare meting!
I have holden my heting.
　　　Have a bob of cherys!

Second
Shepherd

Hail, sufferan Savioure,
　For thou has us soght!
Hail, frely foyde and floure,
　That all thing has wroght!
Hail, full of favoure,
　That made all of noght!
Hail! I kneel and I cowre.
　A bird have I broght
　　　To my barne.
Hail, litel tiné mop!
Of oure crede thou art crop;
I wold drink on thy cop,
　　　Litel day starne.

	Hail, derling dere,
Third	Full of godhede!
Shepherd	I pray thee be nere

Third Shepherd

Hail, derling dere,
　Full of godhede!
I pray thee be nere
　When that I have nede.
Hail! Swete is thy chere;
　My hart woldė blede
To see thee sitt here
　In so poorė wede,
　　With no pennys.
Hail! Put furth thy dall!
I bring thee bot a ball;
Have and play thee with all,
　And go to the tenis!

ANON

From the Second Shepherds' Pageant

"THIS YONDER NIGHT I SAWE A SIGHTE"

This yonder night I sawe a sighte:
A sterre as bright as ony daye;
And ever amonge a maidene songe,
"By by, lully, lullaye."

This maiden hight Mary, she was full milde,
She knelede bifore here owne dere childe.
　She lullede, she lappede,
　She rullede, she wrapped,
　She wepped withoutene nay;
　She rullede him, she dressede him,
　She lissed him, she blessed him,
　She sange: "Dere sone, lullay."

She saide: "Dere sone, ly still and slepe.
What cause hast thu so sore to wepe,
   With sighing, with sobbinge;
   With crying and with scrycchinge,
   All this londe-day;
   And thus wakinge with sore wepinge,
   With many salt teres droppinge?
   Ly stille, dere sone, I thee pray."

"Moder," he saide, "for man I wepe so sore
And for his love I shall be tore
   With scorging, with thretning,
   With bobbing, with beting—
   For sothe, moder, I saye—
   And on a crosse full by hanging,
   And to my herte foll sore sticking
   A spere on Good Fridaye."

This maidene aunswerde with hevy chere:
"Shalt thu thus sofere, my swete sone dere?
   Now I morne, now I muse,
   I all gladness refuse—
   I, ever for this day.
   My dere sone, I thee pray,
   This paine thu put away,
   And if it possibil be may."

ANON

A RHEMISH CAROL

When to assure us on our way
The baby Jesus Christ was born
Tell me this you pampered clay
Why he chose what you would scorn?
He could have picked the proudest palace, but
Instead he picked a hut.

That was no place for newly-borns,
Scarce room for two beasts, it appears,
The one of them with long long horns,
The other one with long long ears,
In such a sort of spot he chose to be,
He who is majesty.

His downy cushion was a stone,
His coverlet a bunch of hay,
His body was a tender one
And on a wooden rack it lay,
How do you like that, you whose care begins
With caring for your skins?

Born to a cross that men deny
He dies to settle our arrears,
You people die yet do not die
In the embraces of your dears,
Vinegar's all the drink he has to drain
While you, you have champagne.

ROBERT FINCH

Derived from the poem, written in the dialect of
Burgundy, by Bernard de la Monnoye

THE BURNING BABE

As I in hoarie Winter's night
  Stoode shivering in the snow,
Surpris'd I was with sodaine heate,
  Which made my hart to glow;

And lifting up a fearefull eye,
  To view what fire was neare,
A pretty Babe all burning bright
  Did in the ayre appeare;

Who scorchèd with excessive heate,
  Such floods of teares did shed,
As though his floods should quench his flames,
  Which with his teares were fed:

"Alas," (quoth he), "but newly-borne,
  In fierie heates I frie,
Yet none approach to warme their harts,
  Or feele my fire, but I;

"My faultlesse breast the furnace is,
  The fuell wounding thornes:
Love is the fire, and sighs the smoake,
  The ashes, shame and scornes;

"The fewell Justice layeth on,
  And Mercie blowes the coales,
The metall in this furnace wrought,
  Are men's defiled soules:

"For which, as now on fire I am
  To worke them to their good,
So will I melt into a bath,
  To wash them in my blood."

With this he vanisht out of sight,
  And swiftly shrunk away,
And straight I callèd unto minde,
  That it was Christmasse day.

ROBERT SOUTHWELL

HYMN: THE NATIVITY OF OUR LORD
AND SAVIOUR JESUS CHRIST

Where is this stupendous stranger,
  Swains of Solyma, advise,
Lead me to my Master's manger,
  Shew me where my Saviour lies?

O Most Mighty! O MOST HOLY!
  Far beyond the seraph's thought,
Art thou then so mean and lowly
  As unheeded prophets taught?

O the magnitude of meekness!
  Worth from worth immortal sprung;
O the strength of infant weakness,
  If eternal is so young!

If so young and thus eternal,
  Michael tune the shepherd's reed,
Where the scenes are ever vernal,
  And the loves be love indeed!

See the God blasphem'd and doubted
  In the schools of Greece and Rome;
See the pow'rs of darkness routed,
  Taken at their utmost gloom.

Nature's decorations glisten
  Far above their usual trim;
Birds on box and laurels listen,
  As so near the cherubs hymn.

Boreas now no longer winters
  On the desolated coast;
Oaks no more are riv'n in splinters
  By the whirlwind and his host.

Spinks and ouzles sing sublimely,
  "We too have a Saviour born,"
Whiter blossoms burst untimely
  On the blest Mosaic thorn.

God all-bounteous, all-creative,
  Whom no ills from good dissuade,
Is incarnate, and a native
  Of the very world he made.

CHRISTOPHER SMART

A NATIVITY
1914–18

[Kipling's son John was killed in action on the Western Front in 1915.]

The Babe was laid in the Manger
  Between the gentle kine—
All safe from cold and danger—
  "But it was not so with mine,
                    (With mine! With mine!)
"Is it well with the child, is it well?"
  The waiting mother prayed.
"For I know not how he fell,
  And I know not where he is laid."

A Star stood forth in Heaven;
  The Watchers ran to see
The Sign of the Promise given—
  "But there comes no sign to me.
                    (To me! To me!)
"My child died in the dark.
  Is it well with the child, is it well?
There was none to tend him or mark,
  And I know not how he fell."

The Cross was raised on high;
  The Mother grieved beside—
"But the Mother saw Him die
  And took Him when He died.
                    (He died! He died!)
"Seemly and undefiled
  His burial-place was made—
Is it well, is it well with the child?
  For I know not where he is laid."

On the dawning of Easter Day
  Comes Mary Magdalene;
But the Stone was rolled away,
  And the Body was not within—
                              (Within! Within!)
"Ah, who will answer my word?"
  The broken mother prayed.
"They have taken away my Lord,
  And I know not where He is laid."

"The Star stands forth in Heaven.
  The watchers watch in vain
For Sign of the Promise given
  Of peace on Earth again—
                              (Again! Again!)
"But I know for Whom he fell"—
  The steadfast mother smiled,
"Is it well with the child—is it well?
  It is well—it is well with the child!"

RUDYARD KIPLING

BIRTH

In Tommy Morton's byre—
but the child, when it came, was perfect.

Milking the Friesian,
squeezing the softness, pinging the pail—

soft chandelier of stalactites:
the shifting legs prop up the hundredweights of dark.

And the waters broke in a little beck:
it helter-skelters slowly,

round and down my only pair of tights,
gets inside my overshoes.

The wet stone flags and the hiss of the Tilley
breathing in, and always breathing in.

The swallows came and went like carpenters,
their beaks full of twigs. A trickling tap.

But the child, when it came, was perfect.
The funny fossil of the anus,

cloacal curl coiled up in bloodied alabaster,
and the afterbirth dyeing the milk in the pail.

Centuries later the light brought two of the shepherds,
the tall one picking his nose, and Douthwaite smirking.

They ran for a doctor, fetched Joe from the pub,
smelling of drink and brilliantine,

his old straw hat on the back of his head,
the nimbus of its fraying rim.

And Dr Anderson and Dr Smythe
and Dr Middleton, the senior partner,

all three of them came from the pub,
with penicillin, needles, gut.

CRAIG RAINE
From 'Anno Domini'

MEDITATION ON THE NATIVITY

All gods and goddesses, all looked up to
And argued with and threatened. All that fear
Which man shows to the very old and new—
All this, all these have gone. They disappear
In fables coming true.

In acts so simple that we are amazed—
A woman and a child. He trusts, she soothes.
Men see serenity and they are pleased.
Placating prophets talked but here are truths
All men have only praised

Before in dreams. Lost legends here are pressed
Not on to paper but in flesh and blood,
A promise kept. Her modesties divest
Our guilt of shame as she hands him her food
And he smiles on her breast.

Painters' perceptions, visionaries' long
Torments and silence, blossom here and speak.
Listen, our murmurs are a cradle-song,
Look, we are found who seldom dared to seek—
A maid, a child, God young.

ELIZABETH JENNINGS

THE ANIMALS' CAROL

Christus natus est! the cock   Christ is born
Carols on the morning dark.

Quando? croaks the raven stiff   When?
Freezing on the broken cliff.

Hoc nocte, replies the crow   This night
Beating high above the snow.

Ubi? ubi? booms the ox   Where?
From its cavern in the rocks.

Bethlehem, then bleats the sheep   Bethlehem
Huddled on the winter steep.

Quomodo? the brown hare clicks,   How?
Chattering among the sticks.

Humiliter, the careful wren   Humbly
Thrills upon the cold hedge-stone.

Cur? cur? sounds the coot   Why?
By the iron river-root.

Propter homine, the thrush   For the sake of man
Sings on the sharp holly-bush.

Cui? cui? rings the chough   To whom?
On the strong, sea-haunted bluff.

Mary! Mary! calls the lamb   Mary
From the quiet of the womb.

Praeterea ex quo? cries   Who else?
The woodpecker to pallid skies.

Joseph, breathes the heavy shire   Joseph
Warming in its own blood-fire.

Ultime ex quo? the owl   Who above all?
Solemnly begins to call.

De Deo, the little stare   Of God
Whistles on the hardening air.

Pridem? pridem? the jack snipe   Long ago?
From the stiff grass starts to pipe.

Sic et non, answers the fox   Yes and no
Tiptoeing the bitter lough.

Quomodo hoc scire potest?   How do I know this?
Boldly flutes the robin redbreast.

Illo in eandem, squeaks   By going there
The mouse within the barley-sack.

Quae sarcinae? asks the daw   What luggage?
Swaggering from head to claw.

Nulla res, replies the ass,   None
Bearing on its back the Cross.

Quantum pecuniae? shrills
The wandering gull about the hills.   How much money?

Ne nummum quidem, the rook   Not a penny
Caws across the rigid brook.

Nulla resne? barks the dog
By the crumbling fire-log.

Nothing at all?

Nil nisi cor amans, the dove
Murmurs from its house of love.

Only a loving heart

*Gloria in Excelsis! Then
Man is God, and God is Man.*

CHARLES CAUSLEY

"AN ANNIVERSARY APPROACHES: OF THE BIRTH OF GOD"

An anniversary approaches: of the birth of god
In a stable, son of a virgin and a carpenter,
But really issued from loins of omnipotent glory:
A babe, ejected from the thighs, greased in mucus and
    blood,

Weeping with its first breath, suffering the cold air, high
    king
Of the galaxies, and powerless as a fieldmouse.
Over him breathe the oxen; shepherds who have seen a
    star
Honour the obscure event; and, they say, three travelling

Magi, or charlatans. This is the messenger of hope;
The military have been instructed to deal with him.
A wholesale killing, their invariable strategy,
While abolishing a generation, fails of effect.

We are asked to believe all this (it's only to start with).
What a jumble of the impossible and casual,
Of commonplace mixed with violence; ordinary muddle;
The props and characters scruffy; at best unheroic.

Yet accordant with the disposition of things holy
As we understand them; whose epiphanies are banal,
Not very aesthetic; gnomic; unremarkable;
And very much like what we have to put up with daily.

                                    DAVID WRIGHT
                        From "On the Margin"

CHRISTMAS EVE

When cold, I huddle up, foetal, cross
arms:
but in summer, sprawl:

   secret is plain old
surface area,

decreased in winter, retaining: in summer no limbs
     touching—
radiating:
everything is physical:

   chemistry is physical:
   electrical noumenal mind
  is:
(I declare!)

put up Christmas tree this afternoon:
    fell
asleep in big chair: woke up at
3:12 and it
    was snowing outside, was white!

Christmas Eve tonight: Joseph
is looking for a place:
Mary smiles but
    her blood is singing:

    she will have to lie down:
    hay is warm:
some inns keep only
the public room warm: Mary

is thinking, Nice time
    to lie down,
good time to be brought down by this necessity:

I better get busy
and put the lights on—can't find
    extension cord:
Phyllis will be home, will say, The
tree doesn't have any lights!
I have tiny winking lights, too:
    she will like
them: she went to see her mother:

my mother is dead: she is
deep in the ground, changed: if she
rises, dust will blow all over the place and
    she will stand there shining,
smiling: she will feel good:
she will want
to go home and fix supper: first she will hug me:

an actual womb bore Christ,
divinity into the world:
    I hope there are births to lie down to
back
to divinity,
since we all must die away from here:

I better look for the cord:
we're going to
        the Plaza for dinner:
tonight, a buffet: tomorrow there, we'll
    have a big Christmas
dinner:

before I fell asleep, somebody
phoned, a Mr Powell: he asked
        if I wanted to
sell my land
in Mays Landing: I don't know:
I have several pieces, wonder
    if he wants them all,
wonder what I ought to quote:

earth: so many acres of earth:
own:
how we own who are owned! well,
anyway, he won't care
    about that—said he would
call back Monday: I will
tell him something then:
  it's nearly Christmas, now:
they are all going into the city:
some have sent ahead for reservations:
the inns are filling up:

    Christ was born
in a hay barn among the warm cows and the
donkeys kneeling down: with Him divinity
swept into the flesh
    and made it real.

A. R. AMMONS

Poets' Anniversaries

ON THE EVE OF A BIRTHDAY

So on a night when a heavy full moon was low,
Like this, and Venus's sparklings hung
In the opposite empty sky,

I emerged,—not the first; but was heard, I think,
With some stirrings of possible love my sudden
Animal cry.

Small one, small stiff hand in my hand,
I walked with you tonight on the lawn
Under this other such sky:

You named daffodils "daisies", looked much
At the star, then turned till the light of the moon
Caught the white of your eye.

You were pleased. With scent on my hand
From a root I had dug, and had touched,
So was I.

GEOFFREY GRIGSON

BIRTHDAY

Beloved dog, in from the wet
Reeking of earth, licking my face like a flame,
Your red-brown coat and glowing eyes
Clearer than anything in human nature
Tell me I will live another year.

JAMES MERRILL

MARCH THE 3rd

Here again (she said) is March the third
And twelve hours singing for the bird
'Twixt dawn and dusk, from half past six
To half past six, never unheard.

'Tis Sunday, and the church-bells end
With the birds' songs. I think they blend
Better than in the same fair days
That shall pronounce the Winter's end.

Do men mark, and none dares say,
How it may shift and long delay,
Somewhere before the first of Spring,
But never fails, this singing day?

When it falls on Sunday, bells
Are a wild natural voice that dwells
On hillsides; but the birds' songs have
The holiness gone from the bells.

This day unpromised is more dear
Than all the named days of the year
When seasonable sweets come in,
Since now we know how lucky we are.

EDWARD THOMAS

TRISTIA XIII

Look, he is superfluous—for of what use was it to be
                                                    born?—
  My birthday god at his proper time is at hand again.
Hard-hearted, why did you come to the wretched years of
                                                    my exile?
  You should rather have placed a final limit to them.
If you had really cared for me, if you had any shame in
                                                    the slightest,
  You would not have followed behind me out of my
                                                    fatherland,
And in the place where you first acknowledged me, born
                                                    but to evil,
  There you should have attempted to make it the last day
                                                    for me.
And when I was forced to depart from the City you should
                                                    have acted
  As did my own companions and with sad face said to
                                                    me: "Farewell".

What are you doing in Pontus? Surely the anger of Caesar
  Has not sent you as well to the end of the frigid zone?
Of course you expect the usual honours that custom
                                                    requires,
  That a white robe I should be wearing which hangs
                                                    from my shoulders down,
That a smoking altar be decked out and encircled with
                                                    flowering garlands
  And that grains of incense should crackle on flames
                                                    dedicated to you,
And that I should properly offer the pancakes that mark
                                                    the occasion
  Of my birth, and compose with assenting voice my
                                                    favourable prayers?

I am not in such a position, the times are for me most
                                            improper
    That I should show my delight because you have come
                                            to me.
    A burial altar's more fitting, encircled with death's gloomy
                                            cypress,
    And a pyre heaped up for my body with fires ready to
                                            flame.
I do not wish to burn incense which has no effect on
                                            divine ones
    Nor among such dreadful afflictions should my
                                            benedictions arise.
But if there is something that I should ask for upon this
                                            birthday.
    It is this: that you never come back again to these
                                            regions, I beg,
While a part of the world that is almost its end, it is
                                            named the Pontus
    But falsely called Euxine—its meaning is "hospitable"—
                                            holds me.

OVID
From the Latin (trans. L. R. Lind)

REMARKS OF SOUL TO BODY

On the Occasion of a Birthday Party
for Sergio and Alberta Perosa

You've toughed it out pretty well, old Body, done
Your duty, and gratified most of my whims, to boot—
Though sometimes, no doubt, against your better
   judgment,
Or even mine—and are still
Revving over satisfactorily, considering.

Keep doing your duty, yes, and some fine day
You'll get full pension, with your every need
Taken care of, and not a dime out of your own pocket—
Or anybody's pocket, for that matter—for you won't have
Any needs, not with the rent paid up in perpetuity.

But now tonight, to recognize your faithful service,
We've asked a few friends in, with their Bodies, of course—
Many of those Bodies quite charming, in fact—and after
You've drunk and dined, then you and all the other Bodies
Can go for a starlit romp, with the dogs, in the back
   pasture.

And we, the Owners—of Bodies, not dogs, I mean—
We'll sit by the fire and talk things over, remark
The baroque ironies of Time, exchange
Some childhood anecdotes, then on to the usual topics,
The death of the novel, the plight of democracy, and
   naturally, Vietnam.

But let us note, too, how glory, like gasoline spilled
On the cement in a garage, may flare, of a sudden, up.

In a blinding blaze, from the filth of the world's floor.

ROBERT PENN WARREN

"I DON'T REMEMBER ANYTHING
OF THEN"

I don't remember anything of then, down there around the
    magnolias
where I was no more comfortable than I've been since
though aware of a certain neutrality called satisfaction
sometimes

and there's never been an opportunity to think of it as an
    idyll
as if everyone'd been singing around me, or around a tulip
    tree

a faint stirring of that singing seems to come to me in
    heavy traffic
but I can't be sure that's it, it may be some more recent
    singing
from hours of dusk in bushes playing tag, being called in,
    walking
up onto the porch crying bitterly because it wasn't a
    veranda
"smell that honeysuckle?" or a door you can see through
    terribly clearly,
suffocating netting
or more often being put into a brown velvet suit and
    kicked around
perhaps that was my last real cry for myself
in a forest you think of birds, in traffic you think of tires,
    where are you?
in Baltimore you think of hats and shoes, like Daddy did

I hardly ever think of June 27, 1926
when I came moaning into my mother's world
and tried to make it mine immediately
by screaming, sucking, urinating
and carrying on generally
it was quite a day

I wasn't proud of my penis yet, how did I know how to
     act? it was 1936
"no excuses, now"

FRANK O'HARA

From "Ode to Michael Goldberg's Birth and Other Births"

A BIRTHDAY IN HOSPITAL
Written on the Day

Soon I shall be in tears this birthday morning:
Cards are propped up beside me, people come
And wish me happy days. In ceremony
(Even of childish sorts), I can behave,
Look interested, grateful, courteous,
Be to each one who comes a kind of warmth
And so give back not gratitude, but gifts.

Yet I shall cry, no doubt from loneliness,
From being far away from those I love,
Or any reason I can conjure later.
But are the tears themselves, I wonder, still
A sort of ceremony I must follow,
A childish ritual, necessity,
Something expected by the wishers-well?
I've heard of "gift of tears" but did not know,
Until this moment, what the words could mean.

ELIZABETH JENNINGS

THE AUTHOR TO HIS BODY ON THEIR FIFTEENTH BIRTHDAY 29.ii.80

There's never a dull moment in the human body.
The Insight Lady

Dear old equivocal and closest friend,
Grand Vizier to a weak bewildered king,
Now we approach The Ecclesiastean Age
Where the heart is like to go off inside your chest
Like a party favor, or the brain blow a fuse
And the comic-book light-bulb of Idea black out
Forever, the idiot balloon of speech
Go blank, and we shall know, if it be knowing,
The world as it was before language once again;

Mighty Fortress, maybe already mined
And readying to blow up grievances
About the lifetime of your servitude,
The body of this death one talkative saint
Wanted to be delivered of (not yet!),
Aggressively asserting your ancient right
To our humiliation by the bowel
Or the rough justice of the elderly lecher's
Retiring from this incontinence to that;

Dark horse, it's you we've put the money on
Regardless, the parody and satire and
The nevertheless forgiveness of the soul
Or mind, self, spirit, will or whatever else
The ever-unknowable unknown is calling itself
This time around—shall we renew our vows?
How should we know by now how we might do
Divorced? Homely animal, in sickness and health,
For the duration; buddy, you know the drill.

HOWARD NEMEROV

"ARTERIES JUICY WITH BLOOD"

Arteries juicy with blood.
A murmur resounds through the ranks:
—I was born in '94,
I was born in '92 . . .
And, clutching the worn-out year of my birth,
I whisper through anaemic lips:
I was born in the night of January the 2nd and 3rd
In the unreliable year
Of eighteen ninety something or other, and
The centuries surround me with fire

OSIP MANDELSTAM
From *Lines Concerning the Unknown Soldier*
From the Russian (trans. James Greene)

I AM THE LITTLE IRISH BOY

I am the little Irish boy
　　That lives in the shanty
I am four years old today
　　And shall soon be one and twenty
　　I shall grow up
　　And be a great man
　　And shovel all day
　　As hard as I can.

　　Down in the deep cut
　　Where the men lived
　　Who made the Railroad.

For supper
  I have some potato
  And sometimes some bread
  And then if it's cold
    I go right to bed.

I lie on some straw
Under my father's coat

My mother does not cry
And my father does not scold
For I am a little Irish Boy
And I'm four years old.

Every day I go to school
Along the Railroad
It was so cold it made me cry
The day that it snowed.

And if my feet ache
I do not mind the cold
For I am a little Irish boy
And I'm four years old.

HENRY THOREAU

"LOVELIEST OF TREES, THE CHERRY NOW"

Loveliest of trees, the cherry now
Is hung with bloom along the bough,
And stands about the woodland ride
Wearing white for Eastertide.

Now, of my threescore years and ten,
Twenty will not come again,
And take from seventy springs a score,
It only leaves me fifty more.

And since to look at things in bloom
Fifty springs are little room,
About the woodlands I will go
To see the cherry hung with snow.

A. E. HOUSMAN

HERE HAVE I BEEN THESE ONE AND TWENTY YEARS

Here have I been these one and twenty years
Since first to Being's breeze my Soul unfurled
A voyager upon the wavy world
Half idling, half at work:—by empty fears
And emptier hopes, light mirth and fleeting tears
Tacking and tossed forever yet in vain
Now timidly retiring, now again
Carelessly, idly mingling with my peers.
Here have I been and done myself and other
E'en as much evil and as little good
As misused strength and guideless frailty could;
Here am I friendless and without a brother,
With faculties developed to no end,
Heart emptied, and scarce hoping to amend.

ARTHUR HUGH CLOUGH

"HOW SOON HATH TIME, THE SUBTLE THIEF OF YOUTH"

How soon hath Time, the subtle thief of youth,
 Stol'n on his wing my three and twentieth year!
 My hasting days fly on with full career,
 But my late spring no bud or blossom shew'th.
Perhaps my semblance might deceive the truth,
 That I to manhood am arrived so near,
 And inward ripeness doth much less appear,
 That some more timely-happy spirits endu'th.
Yet be it less or more, or soon or slow,
 It shall be still in strictest measure ev'n
 To that same lot, however mean or high.
Toward which Time leads me, and the will of Heav'n;
 All is, if I have grace to use it so,
 As ever in my great Task-Master's eye.

JOHN MILTON

TWENTY-FOUR YEARS

Twenty-four years remind the tears of my eyes.
(Bury the dead for fear that they walk to the grave in
 labour.)
In the groin of the natural doorway I crouched like a tailor
Sewing a shroud for a journey
By the light of the meat-eating sun.
Dressed to die, the sensual strut begun,
With my red veins full of money,
In the final direction of the elementary town
I advance for as long as forever is.

DYLAN THOMAS

BIRTHDAY

Mother, let me congratulate you on
the birthday of your son.
You worry so much about him. Here he lies,
he earns little, his marriage was unwise,
he's long, he's getting thin, he hasn't shaved.
Oh, what a miserable loving gaze!
I should congratulate you if I may
mother on your worry's birthday.
It was from you that he inherited
devotion without pity to this age
and arrogant and awkward in his faith
from you he took his faith, the Revolution.
You didn't make him prosperous or famous,
and fearlessness is his only talent.
Open up his windows,
let in the twittering in the leafy branches,
kiss his eyes open.
Give him his notebook and his ink bottle,
give him a drink of milk and watch him go.

YEVGENY YEVTUSHENKO
From the Russian
(trans. Peter Levi and Robin Milner-Gulland)

POEM IN OCTOBER

It was my thirtieth year to heaven
Woke to my hearing from harbour and neighbour wood
And the mussel pooled and the heron
Priested shore
The morning beckon
With water praying and call of seagull and rook
And the knock of sailing boats on the net webbed wall
Myself to set foot
That second
In the still sleeping town and set forth.

My birthday began with the water-
Birds and the birds of the winged trees flying my name
Above the farms and the white horses
And I rose
In the rainy autumn
And walked abroad in a shower of all my days.
High tide and the heron dived when I took the road
Over the border
And the gates
Of the town closed as the town awoke.

A springful of larks in a rolling
Cloud and the roadside bushes brimming with whistling
Blackbirds and the sun of October
Summery
On the hill's shoulder,
Here were fond climates and sweet singers suddenly
Come in the morning where I wandered and listened
To the rain wringing
Wind blow cold
In the wood faraway under me.

Pale rain over the dwindling harbour
And over the sea wet church the size of a snail
With its horns through mist and the castle
Brown as owls
But all the gardens
Of spring and summer were blooming in the tall tales
Beyond the border and under the lark full cloud.
There could I marvel
My birthday
Away but the weather turned around.

It turned away from the blithe country
And down the other air and the blue altered sky
Streamed again a wonder of summer
With apples
Pears and red currants
And I saw in the turning so clearly a child's
Forgotten mornings when he walked with his mother
Through the parables
Of sun light
And the legends of the green chapels

And the twice told fields of infancy
That his tears burned my cheeks and his heart moved in
mine.
These were the woods the river and sea
Where a boy
In the listening
Summertime of the dead whispered the truth of his joy
To the trees and the stones and the fish in the tide.
And the mystery
Sang alive
Still in the water and singingbirds.

And there could I marvel my birthday
Away but the weather turned around. And the true
Joy of the long dead child sang burning
In the sun.
It was my thirtieth
Year to heaven stood there then in the summer noon
Though the town below lay leaved with October blood.
O may my heart's truth
Still be sung
On this high hill in a year's turning.

DYLAN THOMAS

WRIT ON THE EVE OF MY 32nd BIRTHDAY

A Slow Thoughtful Spontaneous Poem

I am 32 years old
and finally I look my age, if not more.
Is it a good face what's no more a boy's face?
It seems fatter. And my hair,
it's stopped being curly. Is my nose big?
The lips are the same.
And the eyes, ah the eyes get better all the time.
32 and no wife, no baby; no baby hurts,
    but there's lots of time.
I don't act silly any more.
And because of it I have to hear from so-called friends:
"You've changed. You used to be so crazy so great."
They are not comfortable with me when I'm serious.
Let them go to the Radio City Music Hall.

32; saw all of Europe, met millions of people;
      was great for some, terrible for others.
I remember my 31st year when I cried:
"To think I may have to go another 31 years!"
I don't feel that way this birthday.
I feel I want to be wise with white hair in a tall library
      in a deep chair by a fireplace.
Another year in which I stole nothing!
8 years now and haven't stole a thing!
I stopped stealing!
But I still lie at times,
and still am shameless yet ashamed when it comes
      to asking for money.
32 years old and four hard real funny sad bad wonderful
      books of poetry
—the world owes me a million dollars.

I think I had a pretty weird 32 years.
And it weren't up to me, none of it.
No choice of two roads; if there were,
      I don't doubt I'd have chosen both.
I like to think *chance* had it I play the bell.
The clue, perhaps, is in my unabashed declaration:
"I'm good example there's such a thing as called soul."
I love poetry because it makes me love
      and presents me life.
And of all the fires that die in me,
there's one burns like the sun;
it might not make day my personal life,
      my association with people,
      or my behavior toward society,
but it does tell me my soul has a shadow.

GREGORY CORSO

ON MY THIRTY-THIRD BIRTHDAY

Through life's dull road so dim and dirty,
I have dragg'd to three and thirty.
What have these years left to me?
Nothing—except thirty-three.

LORD BYRON

POEM ON HIS BIRTHDAY

In the mustardseed sun,
By full tilt river and switchback sea
    Where the cormorants scud,
In his house on stilts high among beaks
    And palavers of birds
This sandgrain day in the bent bay's grave
    He celebrates and spurns
His driftwood thirty-fifth wind turned age;
    Herons spire and spear.

    Under and round him go
Flounders, gulls, on their cold, dying trails,
    Doing what they are told,
Curlews aloud in the congered waves
    Work at their ways to death,
And the rhymer in the long tongued room,
    Who tolls his birthday bell,
Toils towards the ambush of his wounds;
    Herons, steeple stemmed, bless.

In the thistledown fall,
He sings towards anguish; finches fly
In the claw tracks of hawks
On a seizing sky; small fishes glide
Through wynds and shells of drowned
Ship towns to pastures of otters. He
In his slant, racking house
And the hewn coils of his trade perceives
Herons walk in their shroud,

The livelong river's robe
Of minnows wreathing around their prayer;
And far at sea he knows,
Who slaves to his crouched, eternal end
Under a serpent cloud,
Dolphins dive in their turnturtle dust,
The rippled seals streak down
To kill and their own tide daubing blood
Slides good in the sleek mouth.

In a cavernous, swung
Wave's silence, wept white angelus knells.
Thirty-five bells sing struck
On skull and scar where his loves lie wrecked,
Steered by the falling stars.
And tomorrow weeps in a blind cage
Terror will rage apart
Before chains break to a hammer flame
And love unbolts the dark

And freely he goes lost
In the unknown, famous light of great
    And fabulous, dear God.
Dark is a way and light is a place,
    Heaven that never was
Nor will be ever is always true,
    And, in that brambled void,
Plenty as blackberries in the woods
    The dead grow for His joy.

    There he might wander bare
With the spirits of the horseshoe bay
    Or the stars' seashore dead,
Marrow of eagles, the roots of whales
    And wishbones of wild geese,
With blessed, unborn God and His Ghost,
    And every soul His priest,
Gulled and chanter in young Heaven's fold
    Be at cloud quaking peace,

    But dark is a long way.
He, on the earth of the night, alone
    With all the living, prays,
Who knows the rocketing wind will blow
    The bones out of the hills,
And the scythed boulders bleed, and the last
    Rage shattered waters kick
Masts and fishes to the still quick stars,
    Faithlessly unto Him

Who is the light of old
And air shaped Heaven where souls grow wild
   As horses in the foam:
Oh, let me midlife mourn by the shrined
   And druid herons' vows
The voyage to ruin I must run,
   Dawn ships clouted aground,
Yet, though I cry with tumbledown tongue,
   Count my blessings aloud:

   Four elements and five
Senses, and man a spirit in love
   Tangling through this spun slime
To his nimbus bell cool kingdom come
   And the lost, moonshine domes,
And the sea that hides his secret selves
   Deep in its black, base bones,
Lulling of spheres in the seashell flesh,
   And this last blessing most,

   That the closer I move
To death, one man through his sundered hulks,
   The louder the sun blooms
And the tusked, ramshackling sea exults;
   And every wave of the way
And gale I tackle, the whole world then,
   With more triumphant faith
That ever was since the world was said,
   Spins its morning of praise,

I hear the bouncing hills
Grow larked and greener at berry brown
   Fall and the dew larks sing
Taller this thunderclap spring, and how
   More spanned with angels ride
The mansouled fiery islands! Oh,
   Holier then their eyes,
And my shining men no more alone
   As I sail out to die.

DYLAN THOMAS

BIRTHDAY

It's raining today, a dark rain,
On water and breaking trees. It's cold.
A day for dying and answering questions on.
Only a few dark days like this
I'm half-way through, I'm thirty-five years old.

And if I should die this minute—supposing—
Looking at nothing much, the wall
Between me, the lamp, and the coughing hillside,
How surprised would I be to snap off
Like a twig and go suddenly flying? Hardly at all.

You? With all your sins
Sticking like merde in your hair: And everyone
(Think how many you know already)
Who's got there before you waving like mad
And calling hallo like a wartime railway station?

Something like that. At least for a while.
Things fall away. We might go on—
Speak in a language of poppies and roses
With faces we love. There may be one
Or two we knew as deep as that, or one—

Who takes us and teaches us, and after,
So mixed up together we no longer care
Which is ourself or the other, go flying
As free and as one as a light flash, the fusion
Quick or as long, as irrelevant as a light-year.

It's pretty scary. But what is a soul
If not a big wish in a small fool
If we have one at all? One or two things
Suggest we may. But no more than you
Can I tell today if yesterday's message was true.

And not all of us soon, and none of us surely
Make for the light. It may depend
How thick our eyes go blind in the dazzle
After how deep and dark we dug
A frozen hole we fell through in the end.

The walls are shaking . . . The wind like an Irish
Country portent laughs in the rigging
Of coffin trees pretending it's crying.
Only a few dark days like this
To think how to climb from the hole these days are
    digging.

P. J. KAVANAGH

ON THIS DAY I COMPLETE MY THIRTY-SIXTH YEAR

MISSOLONGHI, 22 JANUARY 1824

I

'Tis time this heart should be unmoved,
Since others it hath ceased to move:
Yet, though I cannot be beloved,
Still let me love!

II

My days are in the yellow leaf;
The flowers and fruits of love are gone;
The worm, the canker, and the grief
Are mine alone!

III

The fire that on my bosom preys
Is lone as some volcanic isle;
No torch is kindled at its blaze—
A funeral pile!

IV

The hope, the fear, the jealous care,
The exalted portion of the pain
And power of love, I cannot share,
But wear the chain.

V

But 'tis not *thus*—and 'tis not *here*—
Such thoughts should shake my soul, nor *now*,
Where glory decks the hero's bier,
Or binds his brow.

VI

The sword, the banner, and the field,
Glory and Greece, around me see!
The Spartan, borne upon his shield,
Was not more free.

VII

Awake! (not Greece—she *is* awake!)
Awake, my spirit! Think through *whom*
Thy life-blood tracks its parent lake,
And then strike home!

VIII

Tread those reviving passions down,
Unworthy manhood!—unto thee
Indifferent should the smile or frown
Of beauty be.

IX

If thou regret'st thy youth, *why live?*
The land of honourable death
Is here:—up to the field, and give
Away thy breath!

X

Seek out—less often sought than found—
A soldier's grave, for thee the best;
Then look around, and choose thy ground,
And take thy rest.

LORD BYRON

THE BIRTHDAY DREAM

At the worst place in the hills above the city
Late at night I was driving   cutting through
The overbalancing slums. There was no soul or body
In the streets. I turned right   then left somewhere
Near the top, dead-ending into a wall. A car
Pulled out and blocked me. Four men detached from it.
I got out too. It was Saturday night   the thrill
Of trouble shimmered on the concrete. One shadow
Had a bottle of wine. I stood and said, say, Buddy,
Give me a drink of that wine   not at all fearing
Shaking   as on anything but dream bones   dream
Feet I would have. He said, We're looking for somebody
To beat up. It won't be me, I said   and took him
By the arm with one hand and tossed him into the air.
Snow fell from the clearness in time for there
To be a snowbank for him to fall into elbow-first.
He got up, holding the wine. This guy is too big,
He said, he is too big for us; get the Professor.
Four of us stood together as the wind blew and the snow
Disappeared   and watched the lights of the city
Shine   some others appearing   among them   some
Going out   and watched the lava-flow of headlights off
In the valley. Like a gunshot in the building next to us
A light went out   and down came a middle-aged man
With a hairy chest; his gold-trimmed track shorts had
YMCA Instructor on them   and I knew it was time
For the arm game. We stretched out on our stomachs
On top of the dead-end wall. On one side was the drop
We had all been looking into   and the other side sank
Away with my car   with the men: two darks lifted
Us toward the moon. We put our elbows on the wall
And clasped palms. Something had placed gold-rimmed
Glasses of wine beside us   apartment lights hung in them
Loosely   and we lay nose to nose at the beginning

Of that ceremony; I saw the distant traffic cross him
From eye to eye. Slowly I started to push   and he
To push. My body grew as it lay   forced against his
But nothing moved. I could feel the blood vessels
In my brow distend   extend   grow over the wall like vines
And in my neck   swell like a trumpet player's: I gritted
Into his impassive face   where the far lights moved   this
   is
What I want   this is what I came for. The city pulsed
And trembled in my arm   shook with my effort   for miles
In every direction   and from far below in the dark
I heard the voices of men raised up in a cry of wild
Encouragement   of terror   joy   as I strained to push
His locked hand down. I could not move him   did not
   want
To move him   would not yield. The world strove with my
   body
To overcome   the highways shuddered   writhed   came
   apart
At the centerline   far below us a silent train went by
A warning light   and slowly from the embodying air was
   loaded
With thousands of ghostly new cars   in tiered racks
The light like pale wine in their tinted windshields.
The culture swarmed around me like my blood
   transfigured
By force. I put my head down and pushed with all my life
And writing sprang under my forehead   onto the concrete:
Graffitti scratched with a nail   a boot heel   an ice pick
A tire iron   a scrap of metal from a stolen car   saying
You are here   and I woke
Entangled with my wife, who labored   pled   screamed
To bring me forth. The room was full of mildness. I was
   forty.

JAMES DICKEY

ON MY FORTIETH BIRTHDAY

When I was forty the stocktaker came
to take stock. He was dressed in black
like that old advertisement for Sandeman's port.
Let me see your books, he said.
I blew the dust off my ledgers
and showed him the blank pages.
These are nothing but blank pages, he said.
Are you trying to be whimsical?
He had the flat voice that BBC announcers use
when they describe calamity.
My plans are still maturing, I said,
I am on the point of doing something important.
An old lady in Port Talbot likes two of my poems
and she's ordered two copies for the library.
I am piling my rubbish against oblivion,
stacking it against the dark.
If you go up to Aberystwyth
you'll find my name mis-spelt in the dust.

He looked at me in contempt
right through to the lack of backbone.
Yes, he said, but what have you *done*?
What have you actually done with your lovely life?
Well, I said, it's like this . . .
I groped for the cudgelled album
where the corpses were kept.

Outside was the switchyard, with the expresses
coming at one another from all directions.
I hadn't heard a bird around here for years.
Loneliness came down like a lid.

I'll be back, old Sandeman said,
you'd better get those pages filled . . .

JOHN TRIPP

ON THIS DAY I COMPLETE MY
FORTIETH YEAR

Although art is autonomous
somebody has to live in the poet's body
and get the stuff out through his head,
        someone has to suffer

especially the boring sociology of it
and the boring history, the class war
and worst of all the matter of good luck,
        that is to say bad luck—

for in the end it is his fault, i.e. your fault
not to be born Lord Byron and saying
there has already been a Lord Byron is no excuse—
        he found it no excuse—

to have a weather board house and a white
paling fence and poinsettias and palm nuts
instead of Newstead Abbey and owls and graves
        and not even a club foot;

above all to miss the European gloom
in the endless eleven o'clock heat among
the lightweight suits and warped verandahs,
        an apprenticeship, not a pilgrimage—

the girl down the road vomiting dimity
incisored peanuts, the bristly boss speaking
with a captain's certainty to the clerk,
        "we run a neat ship here":

well, at forty, the grievances lie around
like terminal moraine and they mean
nothing unless you pay a man in Frognal
        to categorize them for you

but there are two sorts of detritus, one a pile
of moon-ore, the workings of the astonished
mole who breathes through your journalism
        "the air of another planet",

his silver castings are cherished in books and papers
and you're grateful for what he can grub up
though you know it's little enough beside
        the sea of tranquillity—

the second sort is a catalogue of bitterness,
just samples of death and fat worlds of pain
that sail like airships through bed-sit posters
        and never burst or deflate;

far more real than a screaming letter,
more embarrassing than an unopened statement
from the bank, more memorable than a small
        dishonesty to a parent—

but to make a resolution will not help,
Greece needs liberating but not by me,
I am likely to find my Sapphics not verses
        but ladies in Queensway.

so I am piling on fuel for the dark,
jamming the pilgrims on tubular chairs
while the NHS doctor checks my canals,
        my ports and my purlieus,

praying that the machine may work a while
longer, since I haven't programmed it
yet, suiting it to a divisive music
        that is the mind's swell

and which in my unchosen way
I marked out so many years ago
in the hot promises as a gift I must follow,
      "howling to my art"

as the master put it while he was still young—
these are the epiphanies of a poor light,
the ghosts of mid-channel, the banging doors
     of the state sirocco.

PETER PORTER

DAY OF RENEWAL

I

Do I prefer to forget it? This middle stretch
Of life is bad for poets; a sombre view
Where neither works nor days look innocent
And both seem now too many, now too few.
They told me as a child that ten was a ripe age
When presents must be useful; which was Progress
But I felt sad to end each fairy story,
Kept turning back to the first page.

Candles increased, then vanished. Where I was born,
Heckled by hooters and trams, lay black to the west
And I disowned it, played a ticklish game
Claiming a different birthplace, a wild nest
Further, more truly, west, on a bare height
Where nothing need be useful and the breakers
Came and came but never made any progress
And children were reborn each night.

Go west and live. Not to become but be.
Still that remains an ideal—or a pretence;
Death is, but life becomes, and furthest westward
The dead must lap fresh blood to recover sense
As Homer rightly thought. Birthdays come round
And the child graduates from milk to meat
And loses count of himself, finding and losing
Visions as quickly lost as found.

As time, so place. This day a year ago
Or thirty years lies rooted in one spot
Which in itself has changed but in our mind
Does not become but is; is what it now is not.
Thus for me Cushendun is war and frustrated
Love, Dieppe an astringent idyl, Lahore
Blood, cholera, flies, blank eyes, becoming forty:
Each birthday placed and each place dated.

Such and such my beginnings, launched and engined
With such and such a tackle of nerve and gland
And steered by such and such taboos and values,
My What and How science might understand
But neither the first nor last page tells the story
And that I am remains just that I am.
The whole, though predetermined to a comma,
Still keeps its time, its place, its glory.

* * * *

And so for all of us. Bits and pieces,
Mayoral banquet and barefoot mile,
Here the self-licensed purr of a cat
And there the toasts, the commercial phrases:
This year? Next year? When will you pay me?
Ever and always. Long may he live!
But the clappers overlap in the waves
And the words are lost on the wind. Five farthings . . .
Five farthings for what? For turtles? Candles?
The great procession comes once a year
Like Christmasses, birthdays. Gifts and leases;
They all run out. As a man's wardrobe
Bulges with clothes he no longer wears
Or only on off days; turned again,
Turned and returned, darned and patched,
Stained with memories. Moth and clock
Have done their damn'dest. Ancient brogues
Caught in a wrinkled grin when the wind changed
Repeat their inglenook yarns, remember
Only one walk out of many; a hat
With a bent black brim remembers a funeral;
And white drills drill in India. Memories
Flitter and champ in a dark cupboard
While in a box among old tin whistles
And paper caps lie stubs of candles
Twisted, snuffed out, still in their holders,
Relics of Christmas, birthday butts.
Ding! Dong! Pussy's in the ding-dong!
Who put us here? The daily Why,
The birthday But. We are still children;
Don't Care was hung, Did Care was haunted;
Big A, Little A, Why's in the cupboard;
Why, say the children, is Why in the cupboard?

And what is that light at the top of the well?
Who'll pull us out? We want that light
As the top of the well. On my next birthday
Shall I get out? Or the one after next?
Or the next after that? Or the next after that?
Here come the candles; now can I do it?
The light up above us is one big candle.
To light us to what? To what, say the doubting
Children and stay but not for an answer.
Ding! Dong! What? Ding! Dong! Why?

III

Milestones, My own; small things lost in a vast
Forest of marble obelisks, private code-words
Drowned in a maelstrom of wavelengths. The lines are
    crossed;
The miles are a wrong number; the rivers are jammed
With angry logs on which in great spiked boots
Lumberjacks fight each other and when one falls
They stamp upon his face. While on the shore
The self withdraws to its third floor back, shakes out
Its fears, hopes, hungers, loves, its doubts and visions,
The small things that are its own; which tinkle, sparkle,
Then roll off into corners. What is now?
The corners maybe but the light they danced in
Came through the window, the same light that still
Gilds the murderous river, catches the spikes
On the boot that is raised to blind. So what is own?
One's birthday is a day that people die on—
Shorthand of wavering shadow on white icing
Scribbled by tiny candles. Thus for me
Being twenty-one was at home but seemed at large
For all the coming slump. And being thirty
Was London and the fear of growing old,
Also the fear of war. And being forty

Was an arm sore from the needle, a Tom Collins
In the garden of Faletti's with Lilac Time
Tinkling between the massacres, was Lahore
When all the lines were dead. And now I am forty-three,
At sea in the small hours heading west from the island
Where other massacres drove poor folk west
To make this Turkish delight, so soft and sweet
It lights up one's bad tooth. In the small dark hours
At sea this time and westwards—west to live
A small hour though my own. But next time? (What
Are those lights ahead? Already the port so loved
By Themistocles, great patriot and statesman,
Great traitor five years on?) But next time what? . . .

LOUIS MACNEICE

BIRTHDAY

We have a dog named "Here";
the tame half wags; the bitter
half will freeze, paw still,
and look at the place the world came from.
I have explored Here's shoulder,
patting it. There is a muscle there
that levels mountains, or forbids.

The weather is telling Here a north story:
someone is lost in a waver of peaks in snow,
and only he gets the signal, tired;
has to turn north, even to teeth of the wind—
that is the only road to go,
through storm dark, by seams in the rock, peering.
Someone is always calling out in the snow.

Here stands by me. I am forty-five,
deep in a story strongly told. I've turned;
I know I will again—a straightness
never quite attained. The curve I try
to find becomes a late intention.
I pat Here's shoulder sometimes,
and we watch the clear sky bend.

WILLIAM STAFFORD

"TODAY, THE TWENTY-SIXTH OF FEBRUARY"

Today, the twenty-sixth of February,
   I, half-way to the minute through
The only life I want to know,
   Intend to end this rather dreary
Joke of an autobiography.
   Thirty-five years is quite enough
Of one's own company. I grow
   A bit sick of the terrestrial stuff.

And the celestial nonsense. Swill
   Guzzle and copulate and guzzle
And copulate and swill until
   You break up like a jigsaw puzzle
Shattered with smiles. The idiotic
   Beatitude of the sow in summer
Conceals a gibbering neurotic
   Sowing hot oats to get warmer.

Look on your handwork, Adam, now
    As I on mine, and do not weep.
The detritus is us. But how
    Could you and I ever hope to keep
That glittering sibyl bright who first
    Confided to us, perfect, once,
The difference between the best and the worst?
    That vision is our innocence.

But we shall step into our grave
    Not utterly divested of
The innocence our nativity
    Embodies a god in. O bear,
Inheritors, all that you have,
    The sense of good, with much care
Through the dirty street of life
    And the gutter of our indignity.

I sense the trembling in my hand
    Of that which will not ever lower
Its bright and pineal eye and wing
    To any irony, nor surrender
The dominion of my understanding
    To that Apollyonic power
Which, like the midnight whispering
    Sea, surrounds us with dark splendour.

Enisled and visionary, mad,
    Alive in the catacomb of the heart,
O lonely diviner, lovely diviner, impart
    The knowledge of the good and the bad
To us in our need. Emblazon
    Our instincts upon your illumination
So that the rot's revealed, and the reason
    Shown crucified upon our desolation.

You, all whom I coldly took
    And hid my head and horns among,
Shall go caterwauling down with me
    Like a frenzy of chained doves. For, look!
We wailing ride down eternity
    Tongue-tied together. We belong
To those with whom we shook the suck
    And dared an antichrist to be.

Get rags, get rags, all angels, all
    Laws, all principles, all deities,
Get rags, come down and suffocate
    The orphan in its flaming cradle,
Snuff the game and the candle, for our state
    —Insufferable among mysteries—
Makes the worms weep. Abate, abate
    Your justice. Execute us with mercies!

GEORGE BARKER

From "The True Confession of George Barker"

LINES WRITTEN IN DEJECTION

When have I last looked on
The round green eyes and the long wavering bodies
Of the dark leopards of the moon?
All the wild witches, those most noble ladies,
For all their broom-sticks and their tears,
Their angry tears, are gone.
The holy centaurs of the hills are vanished;
I have nothing but the embittered sun;
Banished heroic mother moon and vanished,
And now that I have come to fifty years
I must endure the timid sun.

W. B. YEATS

WHAT FIFTY SAID

When I was young my teachers were the old.
I gave up fire for form till I was cold.
I suffered like a metal being cast.
I went to school to age to learn the past.

Now I am old my teachers are the young.
What can't be molded must be cracked and sprung.
I strain at lessons fit to start a suture.
I go to school to youth to learn the future.

ROBERT FROST

A BIRTHDAY

I never felt so much
Since I have felt at all
The tingling smell and touch
Of dogrose and sweet briar,
Nettles against the wall,
All sours and sweets that grow
Together or apart
In hedge or marsh or ditch.
I gather to my heart
Beast, insect, flower, earth, water, fire,
In absolute desire,
As fifty years ago.

Acceptance, gratitude:
The first look and the last
When all between has passed
Restore ingenuous good
That seeks no personal end,
Nor strives to mar or mend.
Before I touched the food
Sweetness ensnared my tongue;
Before I saw the wood
I loved each nook and bend,
The track going right and wrong;
Before I took the road
Direction ravished my soul.
Now that I can discern
It whole or almost whole,
Acceptance and gratitude
Like travellers return
And stand where first they stood.

EDWIN MUIR

ODE TO ME

Fifty today, old lad?
Well, that's not doing so bad:
All those years without
Being really buggered about.
The next fifty won't be so good.
True, but for now—touch wood—
You can eat and booze and the rest of it,
Still get a lot of the best of it,
While the shags with fifty or so
Actual years to go
Will find most of them tougher,
The going a good bit rougher
Within the Soviet sphere—
Which means when the bastards are here,
Making it perfectly clear
That all that double-think
(Both systems on the blink,
East and West the same,
And war just the name of a game)
Is the ballocks it always was.
But will it be clear? Because
After a whole generation
Of phasing out education,
Throwing the past away,
Letting the language decay,
And expanding the general mind
Till it bursts, we might well find
That it wouldn't make much odds
To the poor semi-sentient sods
Shuffling round England then
That they've lost what made them men.
So bloody good luck to you, mate,
That you weren't born too late
For at least a chance of happiness,

Before unchangeable crappiness
Spreads over all the land.
Be glad you're fifty—and
That you got there while things were nice,
In a world worth looking at twice.
So here's wishing you many more years,
But not all that many. Cheers!

KINGSLEY AMIS

SPOT-CHECK AT FIFTY

I sit on a hard bench in the park;
The spendthrift sun throws down its gold.
The wind is strong but not too cold.
Daffodils shimmy, jerk and peck.

Two dogs like paper bags are blown
Fast and tumbling across the green;
Far off laborious lorries groan.
I am not lonely, though alone.

I feel quite well. A spot-check on
The body-work and chassis finds
There's not much wrong. No one minds
At fifty going the speed one can.

No gouty twinge in toe, all limbs
Obedient to such mild demands
I make. A hunger-pang reminds
I can indulge most gastric whims.

Ears savour sounds. My eyes can still
Relish this sky and that girl's legs;
My hound of love sits up and begs
For titbits time has failed to stale.

Fifty scored and still I'm in.
I raise my cap to dumb applause,
But as I wave I see, appalled,
The new fast bowler's wicked grin.

VERNON SCANNELL

A PHOENIX AT FIFTY

At new age fifty
turn inward on old self
and rock on my back in a torn green hammock
deep in a ruined garden
where first the sweet birds sang
behind a white wood cottage
at Montecito Santa Barbara
sunk in sea-vine succulents
under huge old eucalyptrees
wind blows white sunlight thru
A mute ruined statue of a nymph dancing
turns in sun
as if to sing "When day is done"
It is not
A helicopter flies
out of an angle of the sun
its windmill choppers waving
thru the waving treetops

thru which the hot wind blows & blows
pure desire made of light
I float on my back in the sea of it
and gaze straight up into eye-white sky
as into eyes of one beloved whispering
                    "Let
             me
                    in"
Too bright
             too bright!
I close my eyes
lest sun thru such lenses
set me afire
but the blown light batters thru
lids and lashes
I burn and leave
no ashes

Yet will arise
LAWRENCE FERLINGHETTI

TURNING FIFTY

Having known war and peace
and loss and finding,
I drink my coffee and wait
for the sun to rise.

With kitchen swept, cat fed,
the day still quiet,
I taste my fifty years
here in the cup.

236

Outside the green birds come
for bread and water.
Their wings wait for the sun
to show their colours.

I'll show my colours too.
Though we've polluted
even this air I breathe
and spoiled green earth;

though, granted life or death,
death's what we're choosing,
and though these years we live
scar flesh and mind,

still, as the sun comes up
bearing my birthday,
having met time and love
I raise my cup—

dark, bitter, neutral, clean,
sober as morning—
to all I've seen and known—
to this new sun.

JUDITH WRIGHT

"THE THING IS SEX, BEN"

*[Shakespeare died on 23 April 1616;
23 April is also his traditional birthday]*

The thing is sex, Ben. It is that which lives
And dies in us, makes April and unmakes,
And leaves a man like me at fifty-two,
Finished but living, on the pinnacle
Betwixt a death and birth, the earth consumed
And heaven rolled up to eyes whose troubled glances
Would shape again to something better—what?
Give me a woman, Ben, and I will pick
Out of this April, by this larger art
Of fifty-two, such songs as we have heard,
Both you and I, when weltering in the clouds
Of that eternity which comes in sleep,
Or in the viewless spinning of the soul
When most intense. The woman is somewhere,
And that's what tortures, when I think this field
So often gleaned could blossom once again
If I could find her. . . .

                       I am most passionate,
And long am used perplexities of love
To bemoan and to bewail. And do you wonder,
Seeing what I am, what my fate has been?
Well, hark you; Anne is sixty now, and I,
A crater which erupts, look where she stands
In lava wrinkles, eight years older than I am,
As years go, but I am a youth afire
While she is lean and slippered. It's a Fury
Which takes me sometimes, makes my hands clutch out
For virgins in their teens. O sullen fancy!
I want them not, I want the love which springs
Like flame which blots the sun, where fuel of body
Is piled in reckless generosity. . . .
You are most learned, Ben, Greek and Latin know,

And think me nature's child, scarce understand
How much of physic, law, and ancient annals
I have stored up by means of studious zeal.
But pass this by, and for the braggart breath
Ensuing now say, "Will was in his cups,
Potvaliant, boozed, corned, squiffy, obfuscated,
Crapulous, inter pocula, or so forth.
Good sir, or so, or friend, or gentleman,
According to the phrase or the addition
Of man and country, on my honor, Shakespeare
At Stratford, on the twenty-second of April,
Year sixteen-sixteen of our Lord was merry—
Videlicet, was drunk." Well, where was I?—

EDGAR LEE MASTERS
From "Tomorrow is My Birthday"

SELF-PORTRAIT

That resigned look! Here I am,
it says; fifty-nine,
balding, shirking the challenge
of the young girls. Time running out
now, and the soul
unfinished. And the heart knows
this is not the portrait
it posed for. Keep the lips
firm; too many disappointments
have turned the mouth down
at the corners. There is no surgery
can mend those lines; cruelly
the light fingers them and the mind

winces. All that skill,
life, on the carving
of the curved nostril and to no end
but disgust. The hurrying eyes
pause, waiting for an outdistanced
gladness to overtake them.

R. S. THOMAS

BIRTHDAY

A fat sixty-year-old man woke me. "Hello,
Ugly," he said. I nodded. Ugly's easy.
"Why don't you punch yourself in the nose?" I said,
"You look like someone who would look better bloody."
"—And cantankerous," he said. "But just try it:
it's you will bleed." I shrugged. What difference
would that make? Everyone's bleeding something.

He saw me duck out the other side of the shrug.
"Where are you going?"—"Not far enough: I'll be back."
I climbed the maple that grew through our sidewalk once,
and looked at the river with Willy Crosby in it.
A man was diving. Two were in the boat:
one rowing, one working the hooks. The hooker shouted.
I was out of the tree and on the bank—where I'd been

before I remembered wrong. Willy was paler
than all the time I had taken to remember,
but I put on my Scout shirt and went to the wake.
It was better than the Senior Class Play later.
I got the part as the dead boy's best friend.
When his mother and father got tired of keening for
    Willy,
they turned and keened for me. "Oh, John," they wailed,

"your best friend's gone! Oh, Willy, poor John's here!
Come out and play!" I could have been with Willy,
as pale as he. And when he wouldn't come out,
they sang me to him. "Oh, Willy, we bought you a suit!
Oh, Willy, we bought you a bed with new silk sheets!
Oh, Willy, we bought you a house to put the bed in!
The house is too small! Come out and play with John!"

—"Why?" said the fat ugly sixty-year-old man.
"Not that I mind dramatics, but what's the point
of hamming it up without a line to tatter?"
"Goodbye," I said. He smirked. "Well, it's a start:
at least it's a speaking part. But it's not that easy.
I won't be said goodbye to. Not by you."
"No?" I said. "Just wait a little and see

how little it costs to kiss you off, friend. Meanwhile
—hello, Ugly." He nodded. "Ugly's easy.
Easier than climbing a tree that isn't there."
"It's there," I said. "Everything's always there."
"Your lines get better," he said, "but they stay pointless."
I shrugged: "You live by points. . . ." But he stopped me.
"Don't shrug away," he said, "There's nowhere to go."

JOHN CIARDI

"WHEN THE SWORD OF SIXTY COMES NIGH HIS HEAD"

When the sword of sixty comes nigh his head
give a man no wine, for he is drunk with years.
Age claps a stick in my bridle-hand:
substance spent, health broken,
forgotten the skill to swerve aside from the joust
with the spearhead grazing my eyelashes.

The sentinel perched on the hilltop
cannot see the countless army he used to see there:
the black summit's deep in snow
and its lord himself sinning against the army.

He was proud of his two swift couriers:
lo! sixty ruffians have put them in chains.
The singer is weary of his broken voice,
one drone for the bulbul alike and the lion's grousing.

Alas for flowery, musky, sappy thirty
and the sharp Persian sword!
The pheasant strutting about the briar,
pomegranate-blossom and cypress sprig!
Since I raised my glass to fifty-eight
I have toasted only the bier and the burial ground.

I ask the just Creator
so much refuge from Time
that a tale of mine may remain in the world
from this famous book of the ancients
and they who speak of such matters weighing their words
think of that only when they think of me.

FIRDAUSI
(From the Persian trans. Basil Bunting)

MY 71st YEAR

After surmounting three-score and ten,
With all their chances, changes, losses, sorrows,
My parents' deaths, the vagaries of my life, the many
        tearing passions of me, the war of '63 and '4,
As some old broken soldier, after a long, hot, wearying
        march, or haply after battle,
Today at twilight, hobbling, answering company roll-call,
    Here, with vital voice,
Reporting yet, saluting yet the Officer over all.

WALT WHITMAN

BIRTHDAY

Some nine hundred fifty circlings of my moon
i doubt i'll see a thousand
my face lunar now too
strings of my limbs unravelled
trunk weak at the core   like an elm's

worse   the brain's chemistry out of kilter
memory a frayed net
speech a slowing disc the needle jumps

& yet i limp about   insist in fact
on thanking the sky's pale dolphin
for flushing & plumping herself once more
into a pumpkin—
that storybook Moon still in my child mind
too deep for any astronaut to dig out

& stubbornly i praise the Enormous Twist
that set my sun to spinning me
these 26,663 times on the only known planet
that could sprout me

i praise too the great god Luck
that grew me into health
(out of mumps, chicken pox, measles, pneumonia, scarlet
fever, enteritis & a dozen broken bones)
Luck that freed me to roam & write
that gave me a lifetime of friends

some dawns it's true came up with betrayal
failure   rejection   bombs dropping
they taught me only happiness had been
& could be again

Sophocles said it's better not to be born
but he waited till 90 to tell us
at 74 i'm too young to know

so i bless whatever stars
gave me a cheerful father
with a bold heart & a dancing body
who passed me his quick eye & ear
& his faithful love-affair with words

& how can i not be grateful
to a Universe that made
my most enduring mother?
she too valued Luck   but she bet on Pluck
If ever deed of mine achieved
a glint of the unselfish
it was a fallen spark
from her lifetime's fire

when i give my dust to the wind
it will be with thanks
for those fellow earthlings
who forgave or forgot
my onetime wife   our son   our grandsons
& those comrades who held me
steady on cliffs

above all
my gratitude to whatever Is above all
to the young who light my evening sky
& to her   my happiest Happenstance—
if she remember me with love
when she is old
it will be immortality enough

EARLE BIRNEY

HE NEVER EXPECTED MUCH
ON
A CONSIDERATION ON MY EIGHTY-SIXTH BIRTHDAY

Well, World, you have kept faith with me,
　　Kept faith with me;
Upon the whole you have proved to be
　　Much as you said you were.
Since as a child I used to lie
Upon the leaze and watch the sky,
Never, I own, expected I
　　That life would all be fair.

'Twas then you said, and since have said,
   Times since have said,
In that mysterious voice you shed
   From clouds and hills around:
"Many have loved me desperately,
Many with smooth serenity,
While some have shown contempt of me
   Till they dropped underground.

"I do not promise overmuch,
   Child; overmuch;
Just neutral-tinted haps and such,"
   You said to minds like mine.
Wise warning for your credit's sake!
Which I for one failed not to take,
And hence could stem such strain and ache
   As each year might assign.

                              THOMAS HARDY

"TO MY NINTH DECAD I HAVE
TOTTERED ON"

To my ninth decad I have tottered on,
   And no soft arm bends now my steps to steady;
She, who once led me where she would, is gone,
   So when he calls me, Death shall find me ready.

                        WALTER SAVAGE LANDOR

Birthday Greetings

MANY HAPPY RETURNS

[for John Rettger]

Johnny, since today is
February the twelfth when
Neighbours and relations
   Think of you and wish,
Though a staunch Aquarian,
Graciously accept the
Verbal celebrations
   Of a doubtful Fish.

Seven years ago you
Warmed your mother's heart by
Making a successful
   Début on our stage;
Naïveté's an act that
You already know you
Cannot get away with
   Even at your age.

So I wish you first a
Sense of theatre; only
Those who love illusion
   And know it will go far:
Otherwise we spend our
Lives in a confusion
Of what we say and do with
   Who we really are.

You will any day now
Have this revelation;
"Why, we're all like people
    Acting in a play."
And will suffer, Johnny,
Man's unique temptation
Precisely at the moment
    You utter this cliché.

Remember if you can then,
Only the All-Father
Can change the cast or give them
    Easier lines to say;
Deliberate interference
With others for their own good
Is not allowed the author
    Of the play within The Play.

Just because our pride's an
Evil there's no end to,
Birthdays and the arts are
    Justified, for when
We consciously pretend to
Own the earth or play at
Being gods, thereby we
    Own that we are men.

As a human creature
You will all too often
Forget your proper station,
    Johnny, like us all;
Therefore let your birthday
Be a wild occasion
Like a Saturnalia
    Or a Servants' Ball.

What else shall I wish you?
Following convention
Shall I wish you Beauty
    Money, Happiness?
Or anything you mention?
No, for I recall an
Ancient proverb;—Nothing
    Fails like a success.

What limping devil sets our
Head and heart at variance,
That each time the Younger
    Generation sails,
The old and weather-beaten
Deny their own experience
And pray the gods to send them
    Calm seas, auspicious gales?

I'm not such an idiot
As to claim the power
To peer into the vistas
    Of your future, still
I'm prepared to guess you
Have not found your life as
Easy as your sister's
    And you never will.

If I'm right about this,
May you in your troubles,
Neither (like so many
    In the USA)
Be ashamed of any
Suffering as vulgar,
Nor bear them like a hero
    In the biggest way.

All the possibilities
It had to reject are
What give life and warmth to
    An actual character;
The roots of wit and charm trap
Secret springs of sorrow,
Every brilliant doctor
    Hides a murderer.

Then, since all self-knowledge
Tempts man into envy,
May you, by acquiring
    Proficiency in what
Whitehead calls the art of
Negative Prehension,
Love without desiring
    All that you are not.

Tao is a tightrope,
So to keep your balance,
May you always, Johnny,
    Manage to combine
Intellectual talents
With a sensual gusto,
The Socratic Doubt with
    The Socratic Sign.

That is all that I can
Think of at this moment
And it's time I brought these
    Verses to a close;
Happy Birthday, Johnny,
Live beyond your income,
Travel for enjoyment,
    Follow your own nose.

                    W. H. AUDEN

BIRTHDAY POEM

to Christopher Isherwood

August for the people and their favourite islands.
Daily the steamers sidle up to meet
The effusive welcome of the pier, and soon
The luxuriant life of the steep stone valleys,
The sallow oval faces of the city
Begot in passion or good-natured habit,
Are caught by waiting coaches, or laid bare
Beside the undiscriminating sea.

Lulled by the light they live their dreams of freedom;
May climb the old road twisting to the moors,
Play leap frog, enter cafés, wear
The tigerish blazer and the dove-like shoe.
The yachts upon the little lake are theirs,
The gulls ask for them, and to them the band
Makes its tremendous statements; they control
The complicated apparatus of amusement.

All types that can intrigue the writer's fancy,
Or sensuality approves, are here.
And I, each meal-time with the families,
The animal brother and his serious sister,
Or after breakfast on the urned steps watching
The defeated and disfigured marching by,
Have thought of you, Christopher, and wished beside me
Your squat spruce body and enormous head.

Nine years ago, upon that southern island
Where the wild Tennyson became a fossil,
Half-boys, we spoke of books and praised
The acid and austere, behind us only
The stuccoed suburb and expensive school.
Scented our turf, the distant baying
Nice decoration to the artist's wish;
Yet fast the deer was flying through the wood.

Our hopes were set still on the spies' career,
Prizing the glasses and the old felt hat,
And all the secrets we discovered were
Extraordinary and false; for this one coughed
And it was gasworks coke, and that one laughed
And it was snow in bedrooms; many wore wigs,
The coastguard signalled messages of love,
The enemy were sighted from the Norman tower.

Five summers pass and now we watch
The Baltic from a balcony: the word is love.
Surely one fearless kiss would cure
The million fevers, a stroking brush
The insensitive refuse from the burning core.
Was there a dragon who had closed the works
While the starved city fed it with the Jews?
Then love would tame it with his trainer's look.

Pardon the studied taste that could refuse
The golf-house quick one and the rector's tea;
Pardon the nerves the thrushes could not soothe,
Yet answered promptly the no-subtler lure
To private joking in a panelled room,
The solitary vitality of tramps and madmen;
Believed the whisper in the double bed:
Pardon for these and every flabby fancy.

For now the moulding images of growth
That made our interest and us, are gone.
Louder today the wireless roars
Warnings and lies, and it is little comfort
Among the well-shaped cosily to flit,
Or longer to desire about our lives
The beautiful loneliness of the banks, or find
The stoves and resignations of the frozen plains.

The close-set eyes of mother's boy
Saw nothing to be done; we look again:
See Scandal praying with her sharp knees up,
And Virtue stood at Weeping Cross,
The green thumb to the ledger knuckled down,
And Courage to his leaking ship appointed,
Slim Truth dismissed without a character,
And gaga Falsehood highly recommended.

Greed showing shamelessly her naked money,
And all Love's wondering eloquence debased
To a collector's slang, Smartness in furs,
And Beauty scratching miserably for food,
Honour self-sacrificed for Calculation,
And Reason stoned by Mediocrity,
Freedom by Power shockingly maltreated,
And Justice exiled till Saint Geoffrey's Day.

So in this hour of crisis and dismay,
What better than your strict and adult pen
Can warn us from the colours and the consolations,
The showy arid works, reveal
The squalid shadow of academy and garden,
Make action urgent and its nature clear?
Who give us nearer insight to resist
The expanding fear, the savaging disaster?

This then my birthday wish for you, as now
From the narrow window of my fourth floor room
I smoke into the night, and watch reflections
Stretch in the harbour. In the houses
The little pianos are closed, and a clock strikes.
And all sway forward on the dangerous flood
Of history, that never sleeps or dies,
And, held one moment, burns the hand.

W. H. AUDEN

FOR THE FOURTH BIRTHDAY OF MY DAUGHTER

When she opens her eye this morning
    upon her fourth year
    may every fruit and flower
    may every bird and beast
    may every herb and tree
    may every child and every
    holy infant hour
seem in bright presence here
    to exercise this day
    their beneficent power
    so that around her bed
    they stand in clusters and
    choirs hand in hand
singing her welcome here
    and every bright-eyed stellar
    and substellar order

gather around to tell her
all is created for her
all for Raffaella
Raffaella Flora.

FOR PATRICK, AETAT: LXX

[Patrick Balfour, 3rd Baron Kinross]

How glad I am that I was bound apprentice
To Patrick's London of the 1920s.
Estranged from parents (as we all were then),
Let into Oxford and let out again,
Kind fortune led me, how I do not know,
To that Venetian flat-cum-studio
Where Patrick wrought his craft in Yeoman's Row.

For Patrick wrote and wrote. He wrote to live:
What cash he had left over he would give
To many friends, and friends of friends he knew,
So that the "Yeo" to one great almshouse grew—
Not a teetotal almshouse, for I hear
The clink of glasses in my memory's ear,
The spurt of soda as the whisky rose
Bringing its heady scent to memory's nose
Along with smells one otherwise forgets:
Hairwash from Delhez, Turkish cigarettes,
The reek of Ronuk on a parquet floor
As parties came cascading through the door:
Elizabeth Ponsonby in leopard-skins
And Robert Byron and the Ruthven twins,

Ti Cholmondeley, Joan Eyres Monsell, Bridget Parsons,
And earls and baronets and squires and squarsons—
"Avis, it's *ages*! . . . Hamish, but it's *aeons* . . ."
(Once more that record, the Savoy Orpheans).

Leader in London's preservation lists
And least Wykehamical of Wykehamists:
Clan chief of Paddington's distinguished set,
Pray go on living to a hundred yet!

SIR JOHN BETJEMAN

"YOUR BIRTHDAY COMES TO TELL ME THIS"

your birthday comes to tell me this

—each luckiest of lucky days
i've loved, shall love, do love you, was

and will be and my birthday is

E. E. CUMMINGS

"BIRTHDAY OF BUT A SINGLE PANG"

Birthday of but a single pang
That there are less to come—
Afflictive is the Adjective
But affluent the doom—
EMILY DICKINSON

"LEST ANY DOUBT THAT WE ARE GLAD THAT THEY WERE BORN TODAY"

Lest any doubt that we are glad that they were born Today
Whose having lived is held by us in noble Holiday
Without the date, like Consciousness or Immortality—
EMILY DICKINSON

TO AUDEN ON HIS FIFTIETH

Dear Whizz, I remember you at St. Mark's in '39,
Slender, efficient, in slippers, somewhat benign,

Benzedrine taker, but mostly Rampant Mind
Examining the boys with scalpel and tine.

I recall the long talk and the poems-show,
Letters sprinkling through the air all day,

Then you went down and put on Berlioz,
Vastly resonant, full of braggadocio.

I look at your picture, that time, that place,
You had come to defend in the American scene

The idea of something new; you had the odd face
For it, books sprawling on the floor for tea.

It was the time of the *Musée des Beaux Arts*,
Your quick studies of Voltaire and of Melville,

In the rumble seat of my old green Pontiac
I scared you careening through to Concord.

And one time at a dinner party, Auden,
You wolfed your meal before the others were served

Treating the guests to an Intellectual Feast
probably better than any of us deserved.

I remember your candor and your sympathy,
Your understanding, your readiness, your aliveness,

Your stubby fingers like lightning down the pages;
Our ensuing American years that made you thrive.

Now you are back at Oxford, an Oxford don,
Half a century gone into the Abyss of Meaning.

Here's my well-wish on your fiftieth,
You flex a new twist to the spirit's feigning.

RICHARD EBERHART

TO MY MOTHER AT 73

Will you always catch me unaware,
Find me fumbling, holding back? You claim
Little, ask ordinary things, don't dare
Utter endearments much but speak my name
As if you hoped to find a child there,
There on the phone, the same

You tried to quiet. You seem to want the years
Wrapped up and tossed away. You need me to
Prove you are needed. Can you sense the tears
So pent up, so afraid of hurting you?
Must we both fumble not to show our fears
Of holding back our pain, our kindness too?

ELIZABETH JENNINGS

TO MRS THRALE
ON HER COMPLETING HER THIRTY-FIFTH YEAR
AN IMPROMPTU

Oft in Danger yet alive
We are come to Thirty-five;
Long may better Years arrive,
Better Years than Thirty-five!
Could Philosophers contrive
Life to stop at Thirty-five,
Time his Hours should never drive
O'er the Bounds of Thirty-five:
High to soar and deep to dive
Nature gives at Thirty-five;

Ladies—stock and tend your Hive,
Trifle not at Thirty-five:
For howe'er we boast and strive,
Life declines from Thirty-five;
He that ever hopes to thrive
Must begin by Thirty-five:
And those who wisely wish to wive,
Must look on Thrale at Thirty-five.

SAMUEL JOHNSON

ODE
To Sir William Sydney, on his Birth-day

Now that the harth is crown'd with smiling fire,
   And some doe drinke, and some doe dance,
        Some ring,
        Some sing,
   And all doe striue t'aduance
The gladnesse higher:
      Wherefore should I
      Stand silent by,
        Who not the least,
        Both loue the cause, and authors of the feast?
Giue me my cup, but from the *Thespian* well,
   That I may tell to SYDNEY, what
        This day
        Doth say,
   And he may thinke on that
Which I doe tell:
      When all the noyse
      Of these forc'd ioyes,

Are fled and gone,
And he, with his best *Genius* left alone.
This day sayes, then, the number of glad yeeres
Are iustly summ'd, that make you man;
Your vow
Must now
Striue all right wayes it can,
T'out-strip your peeres:
Since he doth lacke
Of going backe
Little, whose will
Doth vrge him to runne wrong, or to stand still.
Nor can a little of the common store,
Of nobles vertue, shew in you;
Your blood
So good
And great, must seeke for new,
And studie more:
Not weary, rest
On what's deceast.
For they, that swell
With dust of ancestors, in graues but dwell.
'T will be exacted of your name, whose sonne,
Whose nephew, whose grand-child you are;
And men
Will, then,
Say you haue follow'd farre,
When well begunne:
Which must be now,
They teach you, how.
And he that stayes
To liue vntill tomorrow' hath lost two dayes.
So may you liue in honor, as in name,
If with this truth you be inspir'd,
So may
This day

Be more, and long desir'd:
And with the flame
Of loue be bright,
As with the light
Of bone-fires. Then
The Birth-day shines, when logs not burne, but
men.

BEN JONSON

CANDIDA

for John Betjeman's Daughter

Candida is one today,
What is there that *one* can say?
One is where the race begins
Or the sum that counts our sins;
But the mark time makes tomorrow
Shapes the cross of joy or sorrow.

Candida is one today,
What is there for me to say?
On the day that she was one
There were apples in the sun
And the fields long wet with rain
Crumply in dry winds again.

Candida is one and I
Wish her lots and lots of joy.
She the nursling of September
Like a war she won't remember.
Candida is one today
And there's nothing more to say.

PATRICK KAVANAGH

TO MY BROTHERS
Written to his Brother Tom on His Birthday

Small, busy flames play through the fresh laid coals.
  And their faint cracklings o'er our silence creep
  Like whispers of the household gods that keep
A gentle empire o'er fraternal souls.
And while, for rhymes, I search around the poles,
  Your eyes are fix'd, as in poetic sleep,
  Upon the lore so voluble and deep,
That aye at fall of night our care condoles.
This is your birth-day, Tom, and I rejoice
  That thus it passes smoothly, quietly.
Many such eves of gently whisp'ring noise
  May we together pass, and calmly try
What are this world's true joys,—ere the great voice,
  From its fair face, shall bid our spirits fly.

JOHN KEATS

BIRTHDAY

If I were well-to-do
I would put roses on roses, and cover your grave
With multitude of white roses, and just a few
    Red ones, a bloody-white flag over you.

So people passing under
The ash-trees of the valley road, should raise
Their eyes to your bright place, and then in wonder
    Should climb the hill, and put the flowers asunder.

And seeing it is your birthday,
They would say, seeing each mouth of white rose praise
You highly, every blood-red rose display
    Your triumph of anguish above you, they would say:

"'Tis strange, we never knew
While she was here and walking in our ways
That she was as the wine-jar whence we drew
    Our draught of faith that sent us on anew."

And so I'd raise
A rose-bush unto you in all their hearts
A rose of memory with a scent of praise
    Wafting like solace down their length of days.

D. H. LAWRENCE

LITTLE BROTHER'S SECRET

When my birthday was coming
Little Brother had a secret:
He kept it for days and days
And just hummed a little tune when I asked him.
But one night it rained
And I woke up and heard him crying:
Then he told me.
"I planted two lumps of sugar in your garden
Because you love it so frightfully
I thought there would be a whole sugar tree for
    your birthday,
And now it will all be melted."
O the darling!

KATHERINE MANSFIELD

UNPOSTED BIRTHDAY CARD

I would like to give you
a thought like a precious stone
and precious stones a thought
couldn't think of.

When you see the lolling tongues
in the shadows, I would like to change them
to gentle candles whose grace
would reveal only yours.

I would like to place you
where the fact of the fairytale
and the fact of the syllogism
make one quiet room
with a fire burning.

I would like to give you
a whole succession of birthdays
that would add up only
to this one: that would be
without years.

NORMAN MACCAIG

16. ix. 65

for Vassili and Mimi

Summer's last half moon waning high
Dims and curdles. Up before the bees
On our friend's birthday, we have left him
To wake in their floating maze.

Light downward strokes of yellow, green, and rust
Render the almond grove. Trunk after trunk
Tries to get right, in charcoal,
The donkey's artless contrapposto.

Sunrise. On the beach
Two turkey gentlemen, heads shaven blue
Above dry silk kimonos sashed with swords,
Treat us to a Kabuki interlude.

The tiny fish risen excitedly
Through absolute transparence
Lie in the boat, gasping and fanning themselves
As if the day were warmer than the sea.

Cut up for bait, our deadest ones
Reappear live, by magic, on the hook.
Never anything big or gaudy—
Line after spangled line of light, light verse.

A radio is playing "Mack the Knife".
The morning's catch fills one straw hat.
Years since I'd fished. Who knows when in this life
Another chance will come?

Between our toes unused to sandals
Each step home strikes its match.
And now, with evening's four and twenty candles
Lit among stars, waves, pines

To animate our friend's face, all our faces
About a round, sweet loaf,
Mavríli brays. We take him some,
Return with honey on our drunken feet.

JAMES MERRILL

BEATRIX IS THREE

At the top of the stairs
I ask for her hand. OK.
She gives it to me.
How her fist fits my palm,
A bunch of consolation.
We take our time
Down the steep carpetway
As I wish silently
That the stairs were endless.

ADRIAN MITCHELL

JOHN BUTTON BIRTHDAY

Sentiments are nice, "The Lonely Crowd",
a rift in the clouds appears above the purple,
you find a birthday greeting card with violets
which says "a perfect friend" and means
"I love you" but the customer is forced to be
shy. It says less, as all things must.
                                        But
grease sticks to the red ribs shaped like a
sea shell, grease, light and rosy that smells of
sandalwood: it's memory! I remember J.A.
staggering over to me in the San Remo and murmuring
"I've met someone MARVELLOUS!" That's friendship
for you, and the sentiment of introduction.

And now that I have finished dinner I can continue.

What is it that attracts one to one? Mystery?
I think of you in Paris with a red beard, a
theological student; in London talking to a friend
who lunched with Dowager Queen Mary and offered
her his last cigarette; in Los Angeles shopping
at the Supermarket; on Mount Shasta, looking . . .
above all on Mount Shasta in your unknown youth
and photograph.
        And then the way you straighten
people out. How ambitious you are! And that you're
a painter is a great satisfaction, too. You know how
I feel about painters. I sometimes think poetry
only describes.
        Now I have taken down the underwear
I washed last night from the various light fixtures
and can proceed.

        And the lift of our experiences
together, which seem to me legendary. The long subways
to our old neighborhood the near East 49th and 53rd,
and before them the laughing in bars till we cried,
and the crying in movies till we laughed, the tenting
tonight on the old camp grounds! How beautiful it is
to visit someone for instant coffee! and you visiting
Cambridge, Massachusetts, talking for two weeks worth
in hours, and watching Maria Tallchief in the Public
Gardens while the swan-boats slumbered. And now,
not that I'm interrupting again, I mean your now,
you are 82 and I am 30. And in 1984 I trust we'll still
be high together. I'll say "Let's go to a bar"
and you'll say "Let's go to a movie" and we'll go to both;
like two old Chinese drunkards arguing about their
favorite mountain and the million reasons for them both.

FRANK O'HARA

TOM SOUTHERNE'S BIRTH-DAY
DINNER AT LD. ORRERY'S

Resign'd to live, prepar'd to die,
With not one sin but poetry,
This day TOM's fair account has run
(Without a blot) to eighty-one.
Kind *Boyle* before his poet lays
A table with a cloth of bays;
And *Ireland*, mother of sweet singers,
Presents her harp still to his fingers,
The feast, his tow'ring genius marks
In yonder wildgoose, and the larks!
The mushrooms shew his wit was sudden!
And for his judgment lo a pudden!
Roast beef, tho' old, proclaims him stout,
And grace, altho' a bard, devout.
May TOM, whom heav'n sent down to raise
The price of prologues and of plays,
Be ev'ry birth-day more a winner,
Digest his thirty-thousandth dinner;
Walk to his grave without reproach,
And scorn a rascal and a coach!

ALEXANDER POPE

"I USED TO WATCH YOU, SLEEPING"

I used to watch you, sleeping,
Your once brown shining ringlets gray.
It was your way to lie
Your knees high, your old twisted hands
In the archaic posture of the unborn,
Raised to your pillow, and I could see
How in the cradle you had lain
For comfort of your own warmth curled up
Like those poor children covered by the robin
With leaves, or under blanket of snow the snowdrop.
Your neglected childhood told its story
In the way you composed yourself for the grave.
Why had not your mother, bending over her baby,
Ninety years ago, wrapped you warm?
I, your daughter, felt pity
For that unwanted babe, for comfort too long ago, too
    far away.

KATHLEEN RAINE
From "My Mother's Birthday"

A BIRTHDAY

My heart is like a singing bird
    Whose nest is in a watered shoot:
My heart is like an apple-tree
    Whose boughs are bent with thickset fruit;
My heart is like a rainbow shell
    That paddles in a halcyon sea;
My heart is gladder than all these
    Because my love is come to me.

Raise me a dais of silk and down;
    Hang it with vair and purple dyes;
Carve it in doves and pomegranates,
    And peacocks with a hundred eyes;
Work it in gold and silver grapes,
    In leaves and silver fleur-de-lys
Because the birthday of my life
    Is come, my love is come to me.

CHRISTINA ROSSETTI

MOVING IN

I wish you for your birthday as you are,
Inherently happy,
The little girl always shining out of your face
And the woman standing her ground.

Wish you the seldom oceanic earthquake
Which shatters your gaze
Against some previous interior past
And rights you

Wish you your honesty normal as a tree
Confounding the caws of intellectuals.
When I zip your dress I kiss you on the neck,
A talisman in honor of your pride.

When I hold your head in my hands
It is as of the roundness of Columbus
Thinking the world, "my hands capable of
Designing the earthly sphere".

Your fingers on the piano keys
Or the typewriter keys or on my face
Write identical transcriptions.
Nothing you do is lost in translation.

I am delighted that you loathe Christmas.
I feel the same way about Communism.
Let us live in the best possible house,
Selfish and true.

May the Verdi *Requiem* continue to knock you out
As it does me; fashionable protest art
Continue to infuriate your heart
And make you spill your drink.

Now ideology has had its day
Nothing is more important than your birthday.
Let us have a solid roof over our head
And bless one another.

KARL SHAPIRO

ON MY WIFE'S BIRTH-DAY

'Tis *Nancy's* birth-day—raise your strains,
Ye nymphs of the Parnassian plains,
And sing with more than usual glee
To *Nancy*, who was born for me.

Tell the blithe Graces as they bound
Luxuriant in the buxom round;
They're not more elegantly free,
Than *Nancy*, who was born for me.

Tell royal *Venus*, though she rove,
The queen of the immortal grove;
That she must share her golden fee
With *Nancy*, who was born for me.

Tell *Pallas*, though th' Athenian school,
And ev'ry trite pedantic fool,
On her to place the palm agree,
'Tis *Nancy's*, who was born for me.

Tell spotless *Dian*, though she range,
The regent of the up-land grange,
In chastity she yields to thee,
O, *Nancy*, who wast born for me.

Tell *Cupid*, *Hymen*, and tell *Jove*,
With all the pow'rs of life and love,
That I'd disdain to breathe or *be*,
If *Nancy* was not born for me.

CHRISTOPHER SMART

STELLA'S BIRTH-DAY, 1718–19

Stella this Day is Thirty-four,
(We shan't dispute a Year or more:)
However *Stella*, be not troubled,
Although thy Size and Years are doubled,
Since first I saw thee at Sixteen,
The brightest Virgin on the Green.
So little is thy Form declin'd;
Made up so largely in thy Mind.

Oh! would it please the Gods, to *split*
Thy Beauty, Size, and Years, and Wit;
No Age could furnish out a Pair
Of Nymphs so graceful, wise, and fair:
With half the Lustre of your Eyes,
With half your Wit, your Years, and Size.
And then, before it grew too late,
How should I beg of gentle Fate,
(That either Nymph might have her Swain,)
To split my Worship too in twain.

JONATHAN SWIFT

STELLA'S BIRTH-DAY, 1726–7

This Day, whate'er the Fates decree,
Shall still be kept with Joy by me:
This Day then, let us not be told,
That you are sick, and I grown old,
Nor think on our approaching Ills,
And talk of Spectacles and Pills.
Tomorrow will be time enough
To hear such mortifying Stuff.
Yet, since from Reason may be brought
A better and more pleasing Thought,
Which can, in spight of all Decays,
Support a few remaining Days:
From not the gravest of Divines,
Accept, for once, some serious Lines.

Although we now can form no more
Long Schemes of Life, as heretofore;
Yet you, while Time is running fast,
Can look with Joy on what is past.

Were future Happiness and Pain,
A mere Contrivance of the Brain,
As *Atheists* argue, to entice,
And fit their Proselytes for Vice:
(The only Comfort they propose,
To have Companions in their Woes.)
Grant this the case; yet sure 'tis hard,
That Virtue, stil'd its own Reward,
And by all Sages understood
To be the chief of human Good,
Should acting, die, nor leave behind
Some lasting Pleasure in the Mind;
Which by Remembrance will asswage
Grief, Sickness, Poverty, and Age:
And strongly shoot a radiant Dart
To shine through Life's declining Part.

Say, *Stella*, feel you no Content,
Reflecting on a Life well spent?
Your skilful Hand employ'd to save
Despairing Wretches from the Grave;
And then supporting with your Store,

Those whom you dragg'd from Death before:
(So Providence on Mortals waits,
Preserving what it first creates)
Your generous Boldness to defend
An innocent and absent Friend:
That Courage which can make you just,
To Merit humbled in the Dust:
The Detestation you express
For Vice in all its glitt'ring Dress:
That Patience under tort'ring Pain,
Where stubborn Stoicks would complain.

   Shall these, like empty shadows, pass,
Or Forms reflected from a Glass?
Or mere Chimæra's in the Mind,
That fly and leave no Marks behind?
Does not the Body thrive and grow
By Food of twenty Years ago?
And, had it not been still supply'd,
It must a thousand times have dy'd.
Then, who with Reason can maintain,
That no Effects of Food remain?
And is not Virtue in Mankind
The Nutriment that feeds the Mind?
Upheld by each good Action past,
And still continu'd by the last:
Then, who with Reason can pretend,
That all Effects of Virtue end?

Believe me, *Stella*, when you show
That true Contempt for Things below,
Nor prize your Life for other Ends,
Than merely to oblige your Friends;
Your former Actions claim their Part,
And join to fortify your Heart.
For Virtue, in her daily Race,
Like *Janus*, bears a double Face;
Looks back with Joy where she has gone,
And therefore goes with Courage on.
She at your sickly Couch will wait,
And guide you to a better State.

O then, whatever Heav'n intends,
Take Pity on your pitying Friends:
Nor let your Ills affect your Mind,
To fancy they can be unkind
Me, surely Me, you ought to spare,
Who gladly would your Suff'rings share:
Or give my Scrap of Life to you,
And think it far beneath your Due:
You, to whose Care so oft I owe,
That I'm alive to tell you so.

JONATHAN SWIFT

DICAMUS BONA VERBA

Speak no evil today, for we honour Cornutus' birth.
Standing here at the altar, be silent, friends!
Burn holy incense now, and from lands at the ends of
   the earth,
burn for their fragrance the spices Arabia sends.
His guardian-spirit comes to receive of us, if he will,
the crown of flowers gathered from bush and vine,
and the nard to bathe his temples—approving, taking his
   fill
of honey-cakes, and drunk on unwatered wine.
Then seize your chance, Cornutus! Now whatever you
   seek
the spirit must grant. Quick, tell your hope! He nods.
It will not be hard to guess your wish before you speak:
your wife's true love. That wish is known to the gods.
No treasure in all the world has a value like this girl's—
not all the wealth the plowman wrests from the fields.
You would not give her up though you were promised
   the pearls
that the great red sea of blessed India yields.
And your prayers are answered. See! Love with a rustle of
   wings
lights at your side with bonds that will keep her there—
golden bonds to endure till slow-paced old age brings
lines to her forehead and cheek, and whitens her hair.

Spirit that saw his birth, make his happiness complete:
bless him with many children to tumble and romp at his
   feet.

TIBULLUS
From the Latin (trans. Constance Carrier)

HAVING REPLACED LOVE WITH FOOD AND DRINK
A Poem for Those who've Reached 40

Sweet basil,
sturdy as my legs, aromatic from Donna's garden, its
   healthy
green leaves pungent
in a fist-sized bouquet on my kitchen sink.

Whirling
the leaves which I have snipped off
as carefully as buttons
in the sharp blades of La Machine,
adding both white fleshes of pine nut and garlic,
a long golden drink of sweet olive oil . . .

A–1 pesto
though I haven't used either mortar or pestle.

My linguini simmers.

This evening alone
with my books
handsome jungle of plants,
real clay:
         Pewabic,
         Grueby,
         Owens,
         Rookwood,
on my shelves.

Yes, I have gladly given up love
for all the objects made with love:

       a poem,
       an orchid,
       this pasta, green and garlicky
       made with my own hands.

                  DIANE WAKOSKI

LITERARY LIFE IN THE GOLDEN WEST
a birthday poem for (and/or about)
Mr J.-L. K. [Jean-Louis (Jack) Kerouac], 20.v.57

Now we are thirty-five we no longer enjoy red neon
          (MILNER HOTEL)
We don't know what to do except
Stand on our head four minutes a day
To adjust our metabolism and feel a physical
Ecstasy when we stand up & the blood
Rushes down from our head

It is impossible to write in the big front room
The space, the high ceiling scares us
In the kitchen we write:

"I have nothing to write about,
no work to do—I made a pastel picture of the backyard
I'm reading *Swann's Way*, I talk to my mother & go see
my friends, they are dull and vaguely busy suffering
from metabolic disturbances (they don't stand on their
heads) I just finished writing a book 1000 pages long.

I'm going away to—or am going to have to
    manufacture—
another world, this one is all worn out, Buddha is much
    more interesting than fucking, eating or writing, my
    mother is happy, now I can die next week."

None of our serious friends approve of this
Routine they write articles against us in all
The liberal magazines, the young hitch-hike from New
    York
And Alabama with their poems, we sit together in
    Portsmouth
Plaza
Drinking muscatel and swapping stories
Until the buttons drive us home.

PHILIP WHALEN

Loyal Greetings

FOR THE QUEEN MOTHER

We are your people;
Millions of us greet you
On this your birthday
Mother of our Queen.
Waves of goodwill go
Racing out to meet you,
You who in peace and war
Our Faithful friend have been.
You who have known the sadness of bereavement,
The joyfulness of family jokes
And times when trust is tried.
Great was the day for our United Kingdoms
And God Bless the Duke of York
Who chose you as his bride.

SIR JOHN BETJEMAN

"TO FORM A JUST AND FINISH'D PIECE"

To form a just and finish'd piece,
Take twenty Gods of Rome or Greece;
Whose godships are in chief request,
And fit your present subject best:
And, should it be your Hero's case,
To have both male and female race,
Your business must be to provide
A score of Goddesses beside . . .

Your Hero now another Mars is,
Makes mighty armies turn their a——s:
Behold his glitt'ring faulchion mow
Whole squadrons at a single blow:
While Victory, with wings outspread,
Flies, like an eagle, o'er his head.
His milk-white steed upon its haunches,
Or pawing into dead men's paunches:
As Overton has drawn his sire,
Still seen o'er many an ale-house fire.
Then from his arm hoarse thunder rolls,
As loud as fifty mustard bowls:
For thunder still his arm supplies,
And light'ning always in his eyes.
They both are cheap enough in conscience,
And serve to echo rattling nonsense.
The rumbling words march fierce along,
Made trebly dreadful in your song.

Sweet poet, hir'd for birth-day rhymes,
To sing of wars chuse peaceful times.
What tho' for fifteen years and more,
Janus hath lock'd his temple-door;
Tho' not a coffee-house we read in
Hath mention'd arms on this side Sweden,
Nor London-Journals, nor the Postmen,
Tho' fond of warlike lies as most men;
Thou still with battles stuff thy head full,
For, must thy hero not be dreadful?

Dismissing Mars, it next must follow
Your conqu'ror is become Apollo:
That he's Apollo is as plain as
That Robin Walpole is Mecænas;
But that he struts, and that he squints,
You'd know him by Apollo's prints.
Old Phœbus is but half as bright,
For yours can shine both day and night;
The first, perhaps, may once an age
Inspire you with poetic rage;
Your Phœbus Royal, ev'ry day,
Not only can inspire, but pay. . . .

Thus your encomium, to be strong,
Must be apply'd directly wrong.
A tyrant for his mercy praise,
And crown a royal dunce with bays:
A squinting monkey load with charms,
And paint a coward fierce in arms.
Is he to avarice inclin'd?
Extol him for his gen'rous mind:
And, when we starve for want of corn,
Come out with Amalthaea's horn.
For all experience this evinces
The only art of pleasing princes. . . .

Now sing his little Highness [Freddy].
Who struts like any king already:
With so much beauty, shew me any maid
That could resist this charming Ganymede?
Where majesty with sweetness vies,
And, like his father, early wise. . . .

May C[arolin]e continue long,
For ever fair and young!—in song.
What tho' the royal carcase must,
Squeez'd in a coffin, turn to dust?
Those elements her name compose,
Like atoms, are exempt from blows.

JONATHAN SWIFT

From "Directions for Making a Birth-Day Song"

"GUID-MORNIN TO YOUR MAJESTY!"

*Thoughts, words and deeds, the Statute blames with reason;
But surely Dreams were n'er indicted Treason.*

*On reading, in the public papers, the Laureate's Ode, with the other
parade of 4 June 1786, the Author was no sooner dropt asleep,
than he imagined himself transported to the Birth-Day Levee; and,
in his dreaming fancy, made the following Address.*

I

Guid-mornin to your MAJESTY!
    May heaven augment your blisses,
On ev'ry new *Birth-day* ye see,
    A humble Poet wishes!
My Bardship here, at your Levee,
    On sic a day as this is,
Is sure an uncouth sight to see,
    Amang thae Birth-Day dresses
                Sae fine this day.

II

I see ye're complimented thrang,
  By many a *lord* an' *lady*;
"God save the King" 's a cukoo sang
  That's unco easy said ay:
The *Poets* too, a venal gang;
  Wi' rhymes weel-turn'd an' ready,
Wad gar you trow ye ne'er do wrang,
  But ay unerring steady,
              On sic a day.

III

For me! before a Monarch's face,
  Ev'n *there* I winna flatter;
For neither Pension, Post, nor Place,
  Am I your humble debtor:
So, nae reflection on YOUR GRACE,
  Your Kingship to bespatter;
There's monie *waur* been o' the Race,
  And aiblins *ane* been better
              Than You this day. . . .

*   *   *   *

V

Far be't frae me that I aspire
  To blame your Legislation,
Or say, ye wisdom want, or fire,
  To rule this mighty nation;
But Faith! I muckle doubt, my SIRE,
  Ye've trusted 'Ministration,
To chaps, wha, in a *barn* or *byre*,
  Wad better fill'd their station
              Than *courts* yon day.

VI

And now Ye've gien auld *Britain* peace,
   Her broken shins to plaister;
Your sair taxation does her fleece,
   Till she has scarce a tester:
For me, thank God, my life's a *lease*,
   Nae *bargain* wearing faster,
Or faith! I fear, that, wi' the geese,
   I shortly boost to pasture
               I' the craft some day.

VII

I'm no mistrusting *Willie Pit*,
   When taxes he enlarges,
(An' *Will's* a true guid fallow's get,
   A Name not Envy spairges)
That he intends to pay your *debt*,
   An' lessen a' your *charges*;
But, G-d-sake! let nae *saving–fit*
   Abridge your bonie *Barges*
               An' *Boats* this day . . .

*   *   *   *

X

For you, young Potentate o' W—,
   I tell your *Highness* fairly,
Down Pleasure's stream, wi' swelling sails,
   I'm tauld ye're driving rarely;
But some day ye may gnaw your nails,
   An' curse your folly sairly,
That e'er ye brak *Diana's pales*,
   Or rattl'd dice wi' *Charlie*
               By night or day.

XI

Yet aft a ragged *Cowte's* been known,
 To mak a noble *Aiver*;
So, ye may dousely fill a Throne,
 For a' their clish-ma-claver:
There, Him at *Agincourt* wha shone,
 Few better were or braver;
And yet, wi' funny, queer *Sir John*,
 He was an unco shaver
    For monie a day.

*   *   *   *

XIV

Ye lastly, bonie blossoms a',
 Ye *royal Lasses* dainty,
Heav'n mak you guid as weel as braw,
 An' gie you *lads* a plenty:
But sneer na *British-boys* awa;
 For Kings are unco scant ay,
An' German-Gentles are but *sma'*,
 They're better just than *want ay*
    on onie day.

XV

God bless you a'l consider now,
 Ye're unco muckle dautet;
But ere the *course* o' life be through,
 It may be bitter sautet:
An' I hae seen their *coggie* fou,
 That yet hae tarrow't at it,
But or the *day* was done, I trow,
 The laggen they hae clautet
    Fu' clean that day.

ROBERT BURNS
From "A Dream"

TO TERRAUGHTY, ON HIS BIRTH-DAY

Health to the Maxwels' veteran Chief!
Health, ay unsour'd by care or grief:
Inspired, I turn'd Fate's sybil leaf,
   This natal morn,
I see thy life is stuff o' prief,
   Scarce quite half-worn.—

This day thou metes threescore eleven,
And I can tell that bounteous Heaven
(The Second-sight, ye ken, is given
   To ilka Poet)
On thee a tack o' seven times seven
   Will yet bestow it.—

If envious buckies view wi' sorrow
Thy lengthen'd days on this blest morrow,
May DESOLATION's lang-teeth'd harrow,
   Nine miles an hour,
Rake them like Sodom and Gomorrah
   In brunstane stoure.—

But for thy friends, and they are mony,
Baith honest men and lasses bony,
May couthie fortune, kind and cany,
   In social glee,
Wi' mornings blythe and e'enings funny
   Bless them and thee:—

Fareweel, auld birkie! Lord be near ye,
And then the deil he daur na steer ye:
Your friends ay love, your faes ay fear ye!
   For me, Shame fa' me,
If neist my heart I dinna wear ye,
   While BURNS they ca' me.

     ROBERT BURNS

CALAIS, AUGUST 15, 1802

Festivals have I seen that were not names:
This is young Buonaparté's natal day,
And his is henceforth an established sway—
Consul for life. With worship France proclaims
Her approbation, and with pomps and games.
Heaven grant that other Cities may be gay!
Calais is not: and I have bent my way
To the sea-coast, noting that each man frames
His business as he likes. Far other show
My youth here witnessed, in a prouder time;
The senselessness of joy was then sublime!
Happy is he, who, caring not for Pope,
Consul, or King, can sound himself to know
The destiny of Man, and live in hope.

WILLIAM WORDSWORTH

ANOTHER PRINCE IS BORN

Fire off the bells, ring out wild guns,
Switch on the sun for the son of sons.
For loyal rubbernecks who wait
Stick a notice on the gate.
Thrill to frill and furbelow,
God Save Sister Helen Rowe.
Lord Evans, Peel, Hall and Sir John
Guard the cot he dribbles on.
An angel in a Hunter jet
Circles round his bassinet.
Inform *The Times*, *Debrett*, *Who's Who*,
Better wake C. Day Lewis too.

Comes the parade of peers and peasants,
The Queen bears children, they bear presents—
Balls and toy guardsmen, well-trained parrots,
A regal rattle (eighteen carats),
And one wise man with myrrh-oiled hair
Brings a six-foot teddy bear
From the Birmingham Toy Fair.

ADRIAN MITCHELL

TO WYSTAN AUDEN
ON HIS BIRTHDAY, 21 FEBRUARY 1967

Now for your sixtieth birthday am I to send you
a long card which is sparkly with greetings?
    Well I might. Or I might in the dark tonight
light sparklers and wave them round in
your honour. Forty years have gone by since I read
a first poem of yours, since you emerged out
of England's life, and her centuries, out of Long Mynd
and her midlands, a poet, also a teacher, in the decentest
sense of the words a "superior person".
("Of course, Grigson, you have only to be with him,
Nicholson, Moore, or MacNeice, a short while,"
the old novelist said—I was young—"to know
they are most superior persons.")
    On TV lately I have seen you amble away
through your orchard under the Alps, seen
your face, wizened, wise, I would say,
slowly divide to a smile benignly lacking
conceit. But I shall not today bow to Tu Fu
in his mountains. Excuse me, instead if I

interfere in your early family concerns and imagine
a choleric baby, wizened, red,
held over a font, and a shell raised, water dribbled,
a voice then in Anglican accent pronouncing "I name
this child Wystan." (That you bawled
would be likely: ex post facto I'm certain in dudgeon
the devil sneaked off through the door.)

Excuse me again if I turn to Thomas of Marlborough,
abbot of Evesham, and read what he says of this
minor saint of our midlands, Wigstan or
Wystan, grandchild of the King of the Men
of the Border—not that you are a saint, I hurriedly say
to save you more and more awkward disclaimer, no one
knowing better than you, though saints may be poets,
poets most seldom are saints.
                    No, but according to Thomas, as you
are aware, this young Wigstan was kissed with
a kiss of peace and then a sword flew, and where
his head of fair hair hit the Wistanstow
field, most strongly, strangely, a pillar of light
came down and stayed there.

By luck, you were named well, and I honour you now as
you've honoured us by your love these long years, still
your head pretty fly on its shoulders, I'm thankful
to say, still in our darkness by rughe knokled knarres
off Main Street, off High Street, by grike
and by fell, an extra fine light, though you
will disclaim that as well.

GEOFFREY GRIGSON

297

YOUR BIRTHDAY IN WISCONSIN
YOU ARE 140

"One of the wits of the school" your chum would say—
Hot diggity!—   What the *hell* went wrong for you,
Miss Emily,—besides the "pure & terrible" Congressman
your paralysing papa.—and Mr Humphrey's dying
        & Benjamin's the other reader? . . .

Fantastic at 32 outpour, uproar, "terror
since September, I could tell to none"
after your "Master" moved his family West
and timidly to Mr Higginson:
        "say if my verse is alive".

Now you wore only white, now you did not appear.
till frantic 50 when you hurled your heart
down before Otis, who would none of it
thro' five years for "Squire Dickinson's cracked daughter"
        awful by months, by hours . . .

Well. Thursday afternoon, I'm in W————
drinking your ditties, and (dear) *they* are *alive,*—
more so than (bless her) Mrs F who teaches
farmers' red daughters & their beaux *my* ditties
        and yours & yours & yours!
        Hot diggity!

                        JOHN BERRYMAN

A LETTER TO DAVID CAMPBELL ON THE BIRTHDAY OF W. B. YEATS, 1965

I

Well, I drink to you, David Campbell, but I drop a curse
  in the cup
For begging a poem on Willy Yeats that took so long
  growing up.
I thought myself safe from rhyming chores, but see I've
  been sold a pup.

A poem for Yeats's birthday? You're organizing a wake
For a boy that's been born a hundred years? Sure, that's a
  piece of cake!
Write it yourself, why don't you? Why don't you jump in
  the lake?

And then I begin to weaken as, of course, I always do;
It's hard to resist you anyway, but the subject tempts me
  too:
That marvellous, monstrous century Yeats didn't quite live
  through.

He was born to the swansdown feeling, when the world
  was wacky and wide;
Tennyson, Browning and Pinch-me went down to swim
  with the tide;
And the Wrath of God descended on Poetry when he
  died.

And in between there was Willy—indeed I loved the man;
Best thing out of Ireland since Tuatha Dè Danaan;
Back of me hand to the warty boys, but I'll write a piece if
  I can.

Sure, I'll write a piece for Willy. It's long time to be dead!
Madame Blavatsky's cuckoo-clock, does he mind now what
    it said:
"Never you rhyme to a ladybird; just keep her warm in
    bed!"

See what a pig of a world it is, the bard was put upon:
Madame Blavatsky's cuckoo turned out to be a swan,
And the swan broke Willy's heart at last, and now he's
    dead and gone.

Now he sleeps with his fathers and minds his p's and q's.
(If it's some of those I could mention, it won't be much of
    a snooze);
But maybe he thinks of other things and cuddles up to the
    Muse.

Is it Dublin Senate he sits in? Does he walk through a
    Dublin school?
Dream of the green-room squabbles or the peaceful lake at
    Coole?
Does he lose himself in the mortal storm with king, beggar
    and fool?

Does he recall the politicos the day he explained his plans
For raising the ghosts of Ireland by spells and talismans
To drive the English into the sea and beat the Black and
    Tans?

Willy was often a prize galah. We musn't say it aloud:
They wouldn't like it in Dublin and we've got to do him
    proud.
So let's dig him up for his hundred years and get him out
    of his shroud.

And not too solemn about it! I know the occasion's grand,
But after all it's his birthday, or so I understand,
And a frock-coated speech to a tombstone was a thing he
  could not stand.

III

What if he talked to the fairies? What if he talked through
  his hat?
The talk itself was magic, and musical magic at that!
And all us sensible fellows, doesn't he leave us flat?

And you and I who are poets, we know the reason why
This is a day for a laughing, not for a weeping, eye:
We go to waken our Master whose bones shall prophesy!

We go to conjure a creature that slouches from its den
Now that the time comes round for the word to be born
  again,
The word that a poet utters, and then becomes, for men.

We are the earth's and of it, but his was the master's spell
That opens a pass to heaven and breaks the jaws of hell;
The tongues of men and of angels—and charity as well!

He was the golden candle that lights man's way to die;
The great shoulder of courage that props a falling sky;
And the voice of intellectual joy we go on living by.

A. D. HOPE

Variations

"LET THE DAY PERISH, WHEREIN
I WAS BORNE"

After this, opened Job his mouth, and cursed his day.
  And Job spake, and said.

Let the day perish, wherein I was borne,
And the night in which it was said, There is a man-childe
  conceived.
Let that day bee darkenesse,
Let not God regard it from above,
Neither let the light shine upon it.
Let darkenes and the shadowe of death staine it,
Let a cloud dwell upon it,
Let the blacknes of the day terrifie it.
As for that night, let darkenesse seaze upon it,
Let it not be ioyned unto the dayes of the yeere,
Let it not come into the number of the monethes.
Loe, let that night be solitarie,
Let no ioyfull voice come therein.
Let them curse it that curse the day,
Who are ready to raise up their mourning.
Let the starres of the twilight thereof be darke,
Let it looke for light, but have none,
Neither let it see the dawning of the day:
Because it shut not up the doores of my mother's wombe,
Nor hid sorrowe from mine eyes.
Why died I not from the wombe?
Why did I not give up the ghost when I came out of the
  bellie?
Why did the knees prevent mee?
Or why the breasts, that I should sucke?
For now should I have lien still and beene quiet,
I should have slept; then had I bene at rest,
With Kings and counsellers of the earth,
Which built desolate places for themselves,

Or with Princes that had golde,
Who filled their houses with silver:
Or as an hidden untimely birth, I had not bene;
As infants which never saw light.
There the wicked cease from troubling:
And there the wearie be at rest.
There the prisoners rest together,
They heare not the voice of the oppressour.
The small and great are there,
And the servant is free from his master.
Wherefore is light given to him that is in misery,
And life unto the bitter in soule?
Which long for death, but it commeth not,
And dig for it more then for hid treasures:
Which reioice exceedingly,
And are glad when they can finde the grave?
Why is light given to a man, whose way is hid,
And whom God hath hedged in?
For my sighing commeth before I eate,
And my roarings are powred out like the waters.
For the thing which I greatly feared is come upon me,
And that which I was afraid of, is come unto me.
I was not in safetie, neither had I rest, neither was I quiet:
Yet trouble came.

From The Book of Job, 3

"HAS ANY ONE SUPPOSED IT LUCKY TO BE BORN?"

Has any one supposed it lucky to be born?
I hasten to inform him or her it is just as lucky to die, and
  I know it.

I pass death with the dying and birth with the new-wash'd
babe, and am not contain'd between my hat and boots,
And peruse manifold objects, no two alike and every one
good,
The earth good and the stars good, and their adjuncts all
good.

I am not an earth nor an adjunct of an earth,
I am the mate and companion of people, all just as
immortal and fathomless as myself.
(They do not know how immortal, but I know.)

Every kind for itself and its own, for me mine male and
female,
For me those that have been boys and that love women,
For me the man that is proud and feels how it stings to be
slighted,
For me the sweet-heart and the old maid, for me mothers
and the mothers of mothers,
For me lips that have smiled, eyes that have shed tears,
For me children and the begetters of children.

Undrape! you are not guilty to me, nor stale nor
discarded,
I see through the broadcloth and gingham whether or no,
And am around, tenacious, acquisitive, tireless, and
cannot be shaken away.

The little one sleeps in its cradle,
I lift the gauze and look a long time, and silently brush
away flies with my hand.

The youngster and the red-faced girl turn aside up the
bushy hill,
I peeringly view them from the top.

The suicide sprawls on the bloody floor of the bedroom,
I witness the corpse with its dabbled hair, I note where the
  pistol has fallen.

WALT WHITMAN
From "Song of Myself"

CHRISTENINGS

The Good Fairies have trooped off one by one,
Their strawberry smiles fading and their
Consumer Durables piled up on the floor.
Here come the Baddies with their stingy gifts,
Small genitals they bring, bow legs, catarrh,
A talent for crosswords and losing girls,
For overhearing insults, getting gossip wrong,
Their Diners Cards make fatherly waiters rude,
What mother says they weep away in bed,
They throw your hat from the ferry when you're drunk:
To us, their godchildren, they give this saw,
A starlight epitaph—*Here they belong*
Who died so young although they lived so long.

PETER PORTER

EXAMINATION AT THE WOMB-DOOR

Who owns these scrawny little feet?   *Death.*
Who owns this bristly scorched-looking face?   *Death.*
Who owns these still-working lungs?   *Death.*
Who owns this utility coat of muscles?   *Death.*
Who owns these unspeakable guts?   *Death.*
Who owns these questionable brains?   *Death.*
All this messy blood?   *Death.*
These minimum-efficiency eyes?   *Death.*
This wicked little tongue?   *Death.*
This occasional wakefulness?   *Death.*

Given, stolen, or held pending trial?
Held.

Who owns the whole rainy, stony earth?   *Death.*
Who owns all of space?   *Death.*

Who is stronger than hope?   *Death.*
Who is stronger than the will?   *Death.*
Stronger than love?   *Death.*
Stronger than life?   *Death.*

But who is stronger than death?
                              Me, evidently.

Pass, Crow.

TED HUGHES

THE SEVEN HOUSES

In Memory of John F. Kennedy

Man, you are at the first door,
The woman receives you.
The woman takes you in.
With joy she takes you in to her long hall.
The nine candles are burning.
Here with reptile and fish and beast
You dance in silence.
Here is the table with the first food.
This is the House of the Womb.

Man, you are at the second door.
A woman receives you.
With brief hands she holds you.
She delivers you into time,
Into light and into darkness,
Into sound and silence and a new dance.
From an outer spring
The natural water comes to your mouth.
Also on your head
A man lays seven bright drops.
This is the House of Birth.

Man, you are at the third door.
A tree in a gray courtyard.
Here the animals dare not enter.
The tree is loaded with apples.
Three women stand at the tree,
The bare bitter bloody tree.
With oil and cloths they stand at the tortured tree.
This is the House of Man.

Man, you are at the fourth door.
Ploughman, merchant, engineer
Cross in a busy street.
On the seven oceans beyond
The ships sail on,
The peoples exchanging oil and wheat and music.
The cornstalk is tall in the field.
Through those yellow tides, that peace,
One woman comes,
On her shoulder a tall jar of untasted wine.
This is the House of Corn and Grape.

Man, you are at the fifth door.
The woman has brought you to her gate.
You have drunk her wine.
She has washed your hands at the threshold.
Now she prepares a bed.
Under the seven stars you watch and wait.
Inside, flames twist and untwist their hair.
This is the House of Love.

Man, you are at the sixth door.
The enemies with sculptured faces,
Stiffly they dance
About the disordered dangerous board.
The broken pitcher spills its oil.
Dark at the wall
The harp is a tangle of strings.
The hungry sit at a narrow table
And the Golden Man
Summons another beast from the flames.
The negro hangs on his tree.
At the sixth wall
In growing darkness, you lit one lamp.
This is the House of Policy.

Man, you are at the last door.
Three small mad venomous birds
Define in your skull
A new territory of silence.
The darkness staggered.
Seventy thousand ordered days
Lay ravelled in the arms of a woman.
In a concord of grief
The enemies laid aside their masks,
And later resumed them

For epitaph, platitude, anger.
What they say is of small importance.
Through the arrogance of atom and planet
May the lamp still burn
And bread be broken at the tables of poor men
(The heads bowed
And the sweet shape of the dove at the door.)
This is the House of History.

GEORGE MACKAY BROWN

SALMON EGGS

The salmon were just down there—
Shuddering together, caressing each other,
Emptying themselves for each other—

Now beneath flood-murmur
They curve away deathwards.
                              January haze,
With a veined yolk of sun. In bone-damp cold
I lean and watch the water, listening to water
Till my eyes forget me

And the piled flow supplants me, the mud-blooms

All this ponderous light of everlasting
Collapsing away under its own weight

Mastodon ephemera

Mud-curdling, bull-dozing, hem-twinkling
Caesarean of heaven and earth, unfelt

With exhumations and delirious advents—

                              Catkins
Wriggle at their mother's abundance. The spider clings to
    his craft.

Something else is going on in the river

More vital than death—death here seems a superficiality
Of small scaly limbs, parasitical. More grave than life
Whose reflex jaws and famished crystals
Seem incidental
To this telling—these toilings of plasm—

The melt of mouthing silence, the charge of light
Dumb with immensity.
                    The river goes on
Sliding through its place, undergoing itself
In its wheel.
                 I make out the sunk foundations
Of burst crypts, a bedrock
Time-hewn, time-riven altar. And this is the liturgy
Of the earth's tidings—harrowing, crowned—a travail
Of raptures and rendings.

                  Sanctus Sanctus
Swathes the blessed issue.

                  Perpetual mass
Of the waters
Wells from the cleft.

               It is the raw vent
Of the nameless
Teeming inside atoms—and inside the haze
And inside the sun and inside the earth.

It is the font, brimming with touch and whisper,
Swaddling the egg.

             Only birth matters
Say the river's whorls.

            And the river
Silences everything in a leaf-mouldering hush
Where sun rolls bare, and earth rolls

And mind condenses on old haws.

                      TED HUGHES

MACDUFF

This wet sack, wavering slackness
  They drew out silent through the long
Blood-edged incision, this black
  Unbreathing thing they must first
Hoist from a beam by its heels and swing
  To see whether it could yet expel
Death through each slimy nostril,
  This despaired-of, half-born mishap
Shuddered into a live calf, knew
  At a glance mother, udder and what it must do
Next and did it, mouthing for milk.
  The cow, too, her womb stitched back inside,
Her hide laced up, leans down untaught
  To lick clean her untimely firstborn:
"Pity it's a male." She looms there innocent
  That words have meanings, but long ago
This blunt lapsarian instinct, poetry,
  Found life's sharpest, readiest
Rhyme, unhesitating—it was knife—
  By some farm-yard gate, perhaps,
That led back from nature into history.

CHARLES TOMLINSON

BIRTH OF RAINBOW

This morning blue vast clarity of March sky
But a blustery violence of air, and a soaked overnight
Newpainted look to the world. The wind coming
Off the snowed moor in the South, razorish,
Heavy-bladed and head-cutting, off snow-powdered ridges.
Flooded ruts shook. Hoof-puddles flashed. A daisy
Mud-plastered unmixed its head from the mud.
The black and white cow, on the highest crest of the
    round ridge,
Stood under the end of a rainbow.
Head down licking something, full in the painful wind
That the pouring haze of the rainbow ignored.
She was licking her gawky black calf
Collapsed wet-fresh from the womb, blinking his eyes
In the low morning dazzling washed sun.
Black, wet as a collie from a river, as she licked him,
Finding his smells, learning his particularity.
A flag of bloody tissue hung from her back-end
Spreading and shining, pink-fleshed and raw, it flapped
    and coiled
In the unsparing wind. She positioned herself, uneasy
As we approached, nervous small footwork
On the hoof-ploughed drowned sod of the ruined field.
She made uneasy low noises, and her calf too
With his staring whites, mooed the full clear calf-note
Pure as woodwind, and tried to get up,
Tried to get his cantilever front legs
In operation, lifted his shoulders, hoisted to his knees,
Then hoisted his back-end and lurched forward
On his knees and crumpling ankles, sliding in the mud
And collapsing plastered. She went on licking him.
She started eating the banner of thin raw flesh that
Spinnakered from her rear. We left her to it.
Blobbed antiseptic on to the sodden blood-dangle

Of his muddy birth-cord, and left her
Inspecting the new smell. The whole South West
Was black as nightfall.
Trailing squall-smokes hung over the moor leaning
And whitening towards us, then the world blurred
And disappeared in forty-five degree hail
And a gate-jerking blast. We got to cover.
Left to God the calf and his mother.

TED HUGHES

TO HELL WITH YOUR FERTILITY CULT

To hell with your Fertility Cult, I
never did want to be fertile,
you think this world is just
a goddamn oversize cunt, don't you? Everything
crowding in and out of it like a railway
terminal   and isn't that nice?
all those people going on trips.
well this is what it feels like, she said,
—and knocked the hen off the nest, grabbed
an egg and threw it at him, right in the face,
the half-formed chick half clung, half slid
half-alive, down over his cheekbone, around
the corner of his mouth, part of it thick
yellow and faintly visible bones and it drippt
down his cheek and chin
—he had nothing to say.

GARY SNYDER

317

MAKE LOVE NOT WAR

Lovers everywhere are bringing babies into the world.
Lovers with stars in their eyes are turning the stars
Into babies, lovers reading the instructions in comic books
Are turning out babies according to the instructions; this
Progression is said by demographers to be geometric and
Accelerating the rate of its acceleration. Lovers abed
Read up the demographers' reports, and accordingly
    produce
Babies with contact lenses and babies diapered in the flags
Of new and underdeveloped nations. Some experts
    contend
That bayonets are being put into the hands of babies
Not old enough to understand their use. And in the US,
Treasury officials have expressed grave concern about
The unauthorized entry of stateless babies without
Passports and knowing no English: these "wetbacks",
As they are called from the circumstance of their
    swimming
Into this country, are to be reported to the proper
Authority wherever they occur and put through channels
For deportation to Abysmo the equatorial paradise
Believed to be their country of origin—"where,"
According to one of our usually unformed sorcerers,
"The bounteous foison of untilled Nature alone
Will rain upon the heads of these homeless, unhappy
And helpless beings apples, melons, honey, nuts, and gum
Sufficient to preserve them in their prelapsarian state
Under the benign stare of Our Lord Et Cetera
    forevermore."

Meanwhile I forgot to tell you, back at the ranch,
The lovers are growing older, becoming more responsible.
Beginning with the mortal courtship of the Emerald
  Goddess
By Doctor Wasp—both of them twelve feet high
And insatiable; he wins her love by scientific means
And she has him immolated in a specially designed
  mole—
They have now settled down in an L-shaped ranch-type
  home
Where they are running a baby ranch and bringing up
Powerful babies able to defend their Way of Life
To the death if necessary. Of such breeding pairs
The average he owns seven and a half pair of pants,
While she generally has three girdles and a stove.
They keep a small pump-action repeater in the closet,
And it will not go off in the last act of this epic.

To sum up, it was for all the world as if one had said
Increase! Be fruitful! Multiply! Divide!
Be as the sands of the sea, the stars in the firmament,
The moral law within, the number of molecules
In the unabridged dictionary. BVD. Amen. Ahem.

                                                    AUM.
(Or, roughly, the peace that passeth understanding.)

                                    HOWARD NEMEROV

Glendower At my nativity
  The front of heaven was full of fiery shapes,
  Of burning cressets, and at my birth
  The frame and huge foundation of the earth
  Shak'd like a coward.
Hotspur   Why, so it would have done
  At the same season, if your mother's cat
  Had but kitten'd, though yourself had never been born.
Glendower I say the earth did shake when I was born.
Hotspur And I say the earth was not of my mind,
  If you suppose as fearing you it shook.
Glendower The heavens were all on fire, the earth did
  tremble.
Hotspur O, then the earth shook to see the heavens on
    fire,
  And not in fear of your nativity.
  Diseased nature oftentimes breaks forth
  In strange eruptions; oft the teeming earth
  Is with a kind of colic pinch'd and vex'd
  By the imprisoning of unruly wind
  Within her womb, which, for enlargement striving,
  Shakes the old beldam earth and topples down
  Steeples and moss-grown towers. At your birth
  Our grandam earth, having this distemp'rature,
  In passion shook.
Glendower   Cousin, of many men
  I do not bear these crossings. Give me leave
  To tell you once again that at my birth
  The front of heaven was full of fiery shapes,
  The goats ran from the mountains, and the herds
  Were strangely clamorous to the frighted fields.
  These signs have mark'd me extraordinary,
  And all the courses of my life do show
  I am not in the roll of common men.

Where is he living, clipp'd in with the sea
That chides the banks of England, Scotland, Wales,
Which calls me pupil, or hath read to me?
And bring him out that is but woman's son
Can trace me in the tedious ways of art
And hold me pace in deep experiments.
Hotspur I think there's no man speaks better Welsh.

WILLIAM SHAKESPEARE
From *Henry IV*, Part I, Act 3, Scene 1

"WHAT DIFFERENT DOOMS OUR BIRTHDAYS BRING!"

Her Birth

What different dooms our birthdays bring!
For instance, one little mannikin thing
   Survives to wear many a wrinkle;
While Death forbids another to wake,
And a son that it took nine moons to make,
   Expires without even a twinkle!

Into this world we come like ships,
Launch'd from the docks, and stocks, and slips,
   For fortune fair or fatal;
And one little craft is cast away,
In its very first trip in Babbicome Bay,
   While another rides safe at Port Natal.

What different lots our stars accord!
This babe to be hail'd and woo'd as a Lord,
    And that to be shunned like a leper!
One, to the world's wine, honey, and corn,
Another, like Colchester native, born
    To its vinegar, only, and pepper.

One is littered under a roof
Neither wind nor water proof,—
    That's the prose of Love in a Cottage—
A puny, naked, shivering wretch,
The whole of whose birthright would not fetch,
Though Robins himself drew up the sketch,
    The bid of "a mess of pottage".

Born of Fortunatus's kin,
Another comes tenderly usher'd in
    To a prospect all bright and burnish'd:
No tenant he, for life's back slums—
He comes to the world as a gentleman comes
    To a lodging ready furnish'd.

And the other sex—the tender—the fair—
What wide reverses of fate are there!
While Margaret, charm'd by the Bulbul rare,
    In a garden of Gul reposes—
Poor Peggy hawks nosegays from street to street,
Till—think of that, who find life so sweet!—
    She hates the smell of roses!

Not so with the infant Kilmansegg!
She was not born to steal or beg,
   Or gather cresses in ditches;
To plait the straw or bind the shoe,
Or sit all day to hem and sew,
As females must, and not a few—
   To fill their insides with stitches!

She was not doom'd for bread to eat
To be put to her hands as well as her feet—
   To carry home linen from mangles—
Or heavy-hearted, and weary-limb'd
To dance on a rope in a jacket trimm'd
   With as many blows as spangles.

She was one of those who by Fortune's boon
Are born, as they say, with a silver spoon
   In her mouth, not a wooden ladle:
To speak according to poet's wont,
Plutus as sponsor stood at her font,
   And Midas rock'd the cradle.

At her first *début* she found her head
On a pillow of down, in a downy bed,
   With a damask canopy over.
For although by the vulgar popular saw,
All mothers are said to be "in the straw",
   Some children are born in clover.

Her very first thought of vital air,
It was not the common chameleon fare
   Of Plebeian lungs and noses,—
      No—her earliest sniff
      Of this world was a whiff
Of the genuine Otto of Roses! . . .

Like other babes, at her birth she cried,
Which made a sensation far and wide,
    Ay, for twenty miles around her;
For though to the ear 'twas nothing more
Than an infant's squall, it was really the roar
    Of a Fifty-thousand Pounder!
      It shook the next heir
      In his library chair,
    And made him cry, "Confound her!"

Of signs and omens there was no dearth,
Any more than at Owen Glendower's birth,
    Or the advent of other great people:
      Two bullocks dropp'd dead,
      As if knock'd on the head,
      And barrels of stout
      And ale ran about,
      And the village-bells such a peal rang out,
    That they cracked the village steeple. . . .

And when she took to squall and kick,
For pain will wring, and pins will prick,
    E'en the wealthiest nabob's daughter;—
They gave her no vulgar Dalby or gin,
But a liquor with leaf of gold therein,
    Videlicet—Dantzic Water.

In short, she was born, and bred, and nurst,
And drest in the best from the very first,
    To please the genteelest censor—
And then, as soon as strength would allow,
Was vaccinated, as babes are now,
With virus ta'en from the best-bred cow
    Of Lord Althorpe's—now Earl Spencer.

THOMAS HOOD
From "Miss Kilmansegg and her Precious Leg"

"A MOST INGENIOUS PARADOX"

Trio—RUTH, KING, and FREDERIC

Ruth

When you had left our pirate fold
 We tried to raise our spirits faint,
According to our customs old,
 With quips and quibbles quaint.
But all in vain the quips we heard,
 We lay and sobbed upon the rocks,
Until to somebody occurred
 A startling paradox.

Fred.
 A paradox?

King (laughing). A paradox!

Ruth

A most ingenious paradox!
We've quips and quibbles heard in flocks,
But none to beat this paradox!
Ha! ha! ha! ha! Ho! ho! ho! ho!

King

We knew your taste for curious quips,
 For cranks and contradictions queer,
And with the laughter on our lips,
 We wished you there to hear.

We said, 'If we could tell it him,
 How Frederic would the joke enjoy!'
And so we've risked both life and limb
 To tell it to our boy.

Fred. (interested). That paradox? That paradox?

King
and } *(laughing).* That most ingenious paradox!
Ruth

We've quips and quibbles heard in flocks,
But none to beat that paradox!
 Ha! ha! ha! ha! Ho! ho! ho! ho!

For some ridiculous reason, to which, however, I've no
    desire to be disloyal,
Some person in authority, I don't know who, very likely
    the Astronomer Royal,
Has decided that, although for such a beastly month as
    February twenty-eight days as a rule are plenty,
One year in every four his days shall be reckoned as
    nine-and-twenty.
Through some singular coincidence—I shouldn't be
    surprised if it were owning to the agency of an
    ill-natured fairy—
You are the victim of this clumsy arrangement, having
    been born in leap-year, on the twenty-ninth of
    February,
And so, by a simple arithmetical process, you'll easily
    discover,
That though you've lived twenty-one years, yet, if we go
    by birthdays, you're only five and a little bit over!
Ruth Ha! ha! ha! ha!
King Ho! ho! ho! ho!
Fred. Dear me!
    Let's see! (*Counting on fingers.*)
    Yes, yes; with yours my figures do agree!
All   Ha! ha! ha! ha! Ho! ho! ho! ho! (FREDERIC *more*
    amused than any.)
Fred. How quaint the ways of Paradox!
    At common sense she gaily mocks!
    Though counting in the usual way,
        Years twenty-one I've been alive,
    Yet, reckoning by my natal day,
        I am a little boy of five!
All   He is a little boy of five! Ha! ha!
    A paradox, a paradox,
    A most ingenious paradox!

Ha! ha! ha! ha! Ho! ho! ho! ho! (RUTH *and* KING
   throw themselves back on seats, exhausted with
   laughter.). . . .

King (rises.) I'm afraid you don't appreciate the delicacy of
   your position. You were apprenticed to us—

Fred. Until I reached my twenty-first year.

King No, until you reached your twenty-first *birthday*
   (producing document), and, going by birthdays,
   you are as yet only five-and-a-quarter.

Fred. You don't mean to say you are going to hold me to
   that?

King No, we merely remind you of the fact, and leave the
   rest to your sense of duty.

Ruth Your sense of duty!

Fred. Don't put it on that footing! As I was merciful to
   you just now, be merciful to me!

W. S. GILBERT

From *The Pirates of Penzance*, Act 2

BRITANNIA'S BABY

Oh Britannia's got a baby, a baby, a baby
Britannia's got a baby, and she got it by and by.

It's called the British Public, the Public, the Public
It's called the British Public, including you and I.

It's such a bonny baby, a baby, a baby
It's such a bonny baby, we daren't let it cry.

So we've got a lot of nurses, of nurses, of nurses
to feed the bonny baby, and keep its tara dry.

   Eat your pap, little man, like a man!
   Drink its minky-winky, then, like a man!

Does it want to go to bye-bye! there then, take its little
                                                  dummy.
take its dummy, go to bye-bye like a man, little man!

Drop of whiskey in its minky? well it shall, yet it shall
if it's good, if it's going to be a *good* little man.

Want to go a little tattah? so it shall, of course it shall
go a banging little tattah with its Auntie
if it's good!
If it's good today, and tomorrow-day as well
then when Sunday comes, it shall go tattah with its Auntie
in a motor, in a pap-pap pap-pap motor, little man!

Oh isn't it a lucky little man!
to have whiskey in its minky
and to go a banging tattah with its Auntie
who loves her little man,
such a dear, kind Auntie, isn't she, to a lucky little
                                                man—!

For Oh, the British Public, the Public, the Public
For Oh, the British Public is a lucky little man!

D. H. LAWRENCE

THE MOTHER'S LULLABY

Hush! lullaby, my baby, nor mix thy tears with mine;
I grieve to think my parents would be no friends of thine;
I grieve to think thy father—oh, grief doth words oppose,
To think thy helpless innocence should find so many foes.

Hush! lullaby, my baby, upon thy mother's arm;
My prayers shall still the storm to rest to leave my baby
  warm,
While to thy father's hall we go, who fast asleep doth lie:
Did he know his door was locked on thee, it might
  unclose his eye.

Hush! lullaby, my baby; he yet thy friend may be,
And by and by I hope to find a friend again in thee;
So hush, my little baby, the day comes by and by,
The storm is gone, the moon is up, so hush and lullaby!

Hush! lullaby, my baby; I wake thee when I sigh,
To think my parents turned their back, nor bade thee one
  "goodbye";
Nor sighed to see thy breath nigh gone, to meet the storm
  so high,
But God has heard, and the storm is gone, so hush and
  lullaby!

JOHN CLARE

TO MY SON

Those flaxen locks, those eyes of blue,
Bright as thy mother's in their hue;
Those rosy lips, whose dimples play
And smile to steal the heart away,
Recall a scene of former joy,
And touch thy father's heart, my Boy!

And thou canst lisp a father's name—
Ah, William, were thine own the same,—
No self-reproach—but, let me cease—
My care for thee shall purchase peace;
Thy mother's shade shall smile in joy,
And pardon all the past, my Boy!

Her lowly grave the turf has prest,
And thou hast known a stranger's breast.
Derision sneers upon thy birth,
And yields thee scarce a name on earth;
Yet shall not these one hope destroy,—
A Father's heart is thine, my Boy!

Why, let the world unfeeling frown,
Must I fond Nature's claim disown?
Ah, no—though moralists reprove,
I hail thee, dearest child of love,
Fair cherub, pledge of youth and joy—
A Father guards thy birth, my Boy!

Oh, 'twill be sweet in thee to trace,
Ere age has wrinkled o'er my face,
Ere half my glass of life is run,
At once a brother and a son;
And all my wane of years employ
In justice done to thee, my Boy!

Although so young thy heedless sire,
Youth will not damp parental fire;
And, wert thou still less dear to me,
While Helen's form revives in thee,
The breast, which beat to former joy,
Will ne'er desert its pledge, my Boy!

LORD BYRON

HER EYES ARE WILD

I

Her eyes are wild, her head is bare,
The sun has burnt her coal-black hair;
Her eyebrows have a rusty stain,
And she came far from over the main.
She has a baby on her arm,
Or else she were alone:
And underneath the hay-stack warm,
And on the greenwood stone,
She talked and sung the woods among,
And it was in the English tongue.

II

"Sweet babe! they say that I am mad,
But nay, my heart is far too glad,
And I am happy when I sing
Full many a sad and doleful thing:
Then lovely baby, do not fear!
I pray thee have no fear of me;
But safe as in a cradle, here
My lovely baby! thou shalt be:
To thee I know too much I owe;
I cannot work thee any woe.

III

"A fire was once within my brain;
And in my head a dull, dull pain;
And fiendish faces, one, two, three,
Hung at my breast, and pulled at me;
But then there came a sight of joy;
It came at once to do me good;
I waked, and saw my little boy,
My little boy of flesh and blood;
Oh joy for me that sight to see!
For he was here, and only he.

IV

"Suck, little babe, oh suck again!
It cools my blood; it cools my brain;
Thy lips I feel them, baby! they
Draw from my heart the pain away.
Oh! press me with thy little hand;
It loosens something at my chest;
About that tight and deadly band
I feel thy little fingers prest.
The breeze I see is in the tree;
It comes to cool my babe and me.

V

"Oh! love me, love me, little boy!
Thou art thy mother's only joy;
And do not dread the waves below,
When o'er the sea-rock's edge we go;
The high crag cannot work me harm,
Nor leaping torrents when they howl;
The babe I carry on my arm,
He saves for me my precious soul;
Then happy lie; for blest am I;
Without me my sweet babe would die.

VI

"Then do not fear, my boy! for thee
Bold as a lion will I be;
And I will always be thy guide,
Through hollow snows and rivers wide.
I'll build an Indian bower; I know
The leaves that make the softest bed:
And if from me thou will not go,
But still be true till I am dead,
My pretty thing! then thou shalt sing
As merry as the birds in spring.

VII

"Thy father cares not for my breast,
'Tis thine, sweet baby, there to rest;
'Tis all thine own!—and if its hue
Be changed, that was so fair to view,
'Tis fair enough for thee, my dove!
My beauty, little child, is flown,
But thou wilt live with me in love;
And what if my poor cheek be brown?
'Tis well for me thou canst not see
How pale and wan it else would be.

VIII

"Dread not their taunts, my little Life;
I am thy father's wedded wife;
And underneath the spreading tree
We two will live in honesty.
If his sweet boy he could forsake,
With me he never would have stayed:
From him no harm my babe can take;
But he, poor man! is wretched made;
And every day we two will pray
For him that's gone and far away.

IX

"I'll teach my boy the sweetest things:
I'll teach him how the owlet sings.
My little babe! thy lips are still,
And thou hast almost sucked thy fill.
—Where art thou gone, my own dear child?
What wicked looks are those I see?
Alas! Alas! that look so wild,
It never, never came from me:
If thou art mad, my pretty lad,
Then I must be for ever sad.

X

"Oh! smile on me, my little lamb!
For I thy own dear mother am:
My love for thee has well been tried:
I've sought thy father far and wide.
I know the poisons of the shade;
I know the earth-nuts fit for food:
Then, pretty dear, be not afraid:
We'll find thy father in the wood.
Now laugh and be gay, to the woods away!
And there, my babe, we'll live for aye."

WILLIAM WORDSWORTH

"LIE EASY IN YOUR SECRET CRADLE"

*Just over against the Muse Gate at Charing-cross is to be seen these Rarities
following, viz. a little Man 3 Foot high, and 32 years of Age, strait and
proportionable every way. The next is his Wife, a little Woman, not 3 Foot
high, and 30 Years of Age, who diverts the Company by her extraordinary
Dancing, and is now big with Child, being the least Woman that ever was
with Child in Europe: Likewise their little Horse, 2 Foot odd Inches high,
which performs several wonderful Actions by the word of Command, being so
small that it's kept in a Box.*

Advertisement in *The Spectator*, Thursday, 13 December 1711.

(The Little Woman addresses the Child in her Womb)
Lie easy in your secret cradle,
my little master.
They come to gape at this small rounded belly,
to judge and grin, to widen yokel eyes
or, oafish, taint the air with filthy jests.

"The least woman that ever was with child."
Does God work miracles in idleness?
Their minds are sealed in large stupidity.
Their eyes are set too far above the ground.

They cannot guess your secret,
little emperor, my secret master. Lie
at anchor in your estuary there.

So many meaty hands upon the rail,
such staring . . . sometimes I have to pity them.
Cast out, disowned, the wrong shape for their size.
Only the cattle should lumber and bellow. Men
were meant in the Creator's mind to be
compact, neat, delicate.
                                    I think of cats,
conies, and hedgehogs in the safe embrace
of our companionable earth.
                                    These oafs have huge noses.
They cannot move with the right human grace.
Sometimes I swear I have to pity them.

Lie easy there,
my hidden conqueror. Grow
through all your comely stages:
                                    first
the size of a sleek mouse: later, the size
of a bright-singing thrush.
                                    Then out, and suck
from these two nipples the milk of our new day!

They pay to stare. It is an idle sport.
If they could know I hold their future here!
My little lord shall drive them howling out.
Already rumours are abroad among them—
a crazed parson has wandered to a country
which he calls Lilliput.

                    Across the seas
are many islands where our people thrive.
It must be so. The parson would not lie.
Their swords flash quick to snip through heavy sinews.
The human-beasts will topple to the earth.
Our cannon will fire too fast for them to count
the shocks that crack their bones.
                              All we have lacked
till now, is our true leader.

                    Madness stalks them.
They cannot keep away from raree-shows.
Curiosity is their illness. To see an oddity
they travel stony miles. This is a sign
they draw towards their end. Blood drowns their sun.

Little prince, this hard world's next emperor,
I have not told your father all my thoughts.
He is a good man, but with specks of blindness.
He does not hate the human-beasts: has friends
among them: says they have done fine things.
Fine things! I feel your scorn laugh in my bones.
All that they make is wrong: too high, too thick.
Their finest houses thrust above the trees,
instead of finding shelter, as they should,
beneath those steady arms. Their music roars
as if in pain. Their cups are chamber-pots.

I do not trust your father with our secret.
One day he will share our happiness. Till then
only one heart beats with this prophecy:
the heart whose thud keeps our two beings warm.

Lie easy in your secret cradle,
my love, my rescuer,
mine and the world's new master:
God does not work His miracles in vain!

It is recorded that Dean Swift was only known to laugh
twice in his life: once when reading Fielding's
Tom Thumb, *and once when watching a juggler.*

(*Sonnet: Dean Swift contemplates the little Woman*)

Maddened by loneliness, a Sybil's heart
in a small animal, shown to boors for pence,
her life one long affront, she draws apart
and in her prayers bulks out their penitence.

Frog-legs kick, moth-wings flutter in her womb.
Deceived by pain, she dreams enormous things:
a gnat's thin trumpet is the blast of doom:
she will be mother to a line of kings.

Her agony is mine, though not her dreams.
My fabled Lilliput was England's truth.
In bitter Ireland now I shun men's sight.

But eyes like hers, where holy hatred gleams
I welcome still: we share one sharp delight,
I in my deanery, she in her booth.

JOHN WAIN
From "Wildtrack"

DOSTOIEVSKY'S DAUGHTERS
1. SOPHIA

Let us now praise famous men; and the children
Whom they begot
By the way, in a frenzy snatched
From the less carnal conceiving
For which we remember them:
Fondly perhaps, not without forethought
At moments, between fits, in the sticky patches between
Turning out copy—bits of *The Idiot*, for instance—
Against time, against better judgment
To catch up with debts generously assumed
In a dead brother's name;
To bloat for a while those insatiable leeches, provide
For dependants close or not close, the helpless or feckless.
Let us praise, too, the women
Who bore with those men, bore their children,
Bore the more carnal labour, rarely remembered.

Sophia they named their first-born
But could not, for weeks, have her christened
In uncongenial Geneva, her mother too ill
To go to the pawnshop as usual.
"The baby," he wrote in March
Of the daughter not one month old,
"Has my features, my expression
Down to the wrinkles on her brow.
She lies in her cot
As though composing a novel."

Ah, yes, paternal. But how could he know
She was composing herself
For wisdom, for moving on?
"So strong, so beautiful,
So full of understanding,
And feeling," he wrote again of the daughter
Lost, not three months old;
And attributed her going

"To the fact that we could not fall in
With the foreign way
Of rearing and feeding babies.'

Praising her now, the forgotten daughter
Wise before she was christened, before she was weaned,
With her brother's wisdom, Myshkin's, and the famous
    man's
Who fathered them both,
Let us remember: somebody has to pay
For goodness—the scandal of it, the affront.
Let us praise, too, the woman.
Between fits, in the sticky patches
The famous man suffered, paid,
But his brainchild, *The Idiot*, lived—
Thanks to her, the carnal mother
Who paid for less carnal conceiving
And paid for the wisdom, the fame
And paid for his paying.

Mourning conceived her, a black soil
Nourished her growth
But when she opened her eyes it was
To a kinder light, to a warmer day.

Love they called her; and gave her the love too
That Wisdom, her sister, had left unused
When she died, in another country.

Did Love thrive on that? She lived longer—
Long enough to see
A baby brother convulsed, choking,
Her famous father parted
From those he loved;
And see him crucified, nailed
Into his coffin, straining—year after year—
For resurrection, so that the light
Might be kind again, a day warm.

No, she could not be Love, but remained
The loved one, Aimée, forsaken;
Before her own blood broke
Must break with her mother, her country
That could not sustain her, since he was gone.

And wrote, the famous man's daughter,
Of doom in the blood,
Of a black soil, mourning,
Of a love that could not redeem
But maimed her, Aimée.

MICHAEL HAMBURGER

CHARLOTTE NICHOLLS

[Charlotte died in March 1855 during this first pregnancy.]

My husband smiles in sleep beside me;
The beck froths happily under Haworth hill,
And moonlight softens the wild tossing heather
On the frosty slopes towards Keighley.
Our coming child has stirred
In my womb, and perhaps I see now
What Emily never saw for the depth
Of her scarred isolation.
Warm truth taps through the decay
Of the artist-urge: a curate's wife, living her vow,
Shames the impassioned fantasy.

If the years of deprivation
Were the years of deepest penetration,
If the sweet fulfilment
Bears me to the shallows, the content
Of common housewives in the village,
And the word that is everybody's word
Replaces the rare scribble on outcast rock—
I still choose the shared fulfilment, trusting
That the loss of the agonized gleam
Is a mere loss of morbidity,
That the bright surface beyond purgation
Holds the abiding poetry.

I serve the Church, console the illiterate,
And learn what the black tempest could not teach,
Here or in Brussels. Emily's speech,
Aloof and cryptic, missed the ultimate
Which I seem to grasp in parish visitation.
In a city or on a moor,
The self-fulfilled alone are really poor.
The voice within the grim shell
Becomes imperious when its new mould is made,
But the friendly echo of a platitude
Uplifts the bereaved, the betrayed,
With fertilizing force denied to art.

I have watched, and fused with, in this parsonage,
Souls complex and original, who must bow
To the pang of finding that the rock-scrawl,
Rasped by the lightning or the ghostly finger,
Is always an extinct text
At faith's true dayspring—a nerve left to smart
In the eroded stoic heart.

I have been released indeed
From that aesthetic bondage
From the fume of fashioning, the loneliness
Of subtle planes where two worlds bleed
On the emerging mirror.
And I am thankful, for the fight was hard,
And Emily's end was terrible. I lie relaxed,
Warmed by my husband, and an owl hoots
Somewhere near the churchyard.
The wind may rise, straining the thorn-roots,
But a calm of ordinary bliss
Bears me to sleep unmarred.

JACK CLEMO

TO MY CHILDREN UNKNOWN, PRODUCED BY ARTIFICIAL INSEMINATION

To my children unknown:
Space projects,
My galactic explosions—
I do not even know
How many of you there are,
If ever you got off the launching pad.

All I know is,
As a "donor"
I received acknowledgement of
"The success of the experiment".
All boys.
Mission completed.

I gave my all.
Under rigid scientific conditions,
In the interests of science I
Was willingly raped:
The exciting suction pump
In a stark laboratory,
Sterile,
Beneath blazing lights,
Masked assistants all eyes.

That laboratory bench
Was the only home I ever made,
My single marriage bed.

A kind of actor, I performed,
Projected my part.
All systems were go.
And come. My role,
The onlie begetter
Of these ensuing
Moppets.

All happiness! Yes—
After the initial mild embarrassment
At making an exhibition of myself
(In front of all those students!)
Despite the public nature of the occasion
And the scientific dispassion
I endured with moody willingness
The blastoff of private pleasure
That sent me to the point of no return
And even beyond,
Back to where I came from,
Into outer space.

My sample deepfrozen, docketed
Even before the almost endless countdown
Of detumescence.
I was advised, clinically speaking,
Not to think of "her"
As "the wife", but only as
"The recipient". The tool
Simply as "the reproductive mechanism",
My essential juices
"Prime sperm" (Caucasian).

On to the Womb, the Moon!
Countdown to zero! Takeoff!
Rockets away! Man in space!
Into orbit! Gee, what a view!
Back to the Womb, the Moon!
To the Lake of Sleep,
The Marsh of Death,
The Sea of Showers.
The trip one long ejaculation . . .

*

Why do I never wonder who you are, wives—
You whose great bowl of a thousand wombs
Bled to a stitch in time?
Even before the nuptial night
Our divorce was final. Could I care much less
About the offspring of my loins, sprigs
Of a poet's side-job? I feel your absence
Only as I might feel amputated limbs.

At least I'm spared

　　　　　　　　The patter of tiny feet.

*

Get lost,
Scions of my poetry, my poverty.
I was well paid to engender you.
(Non-taxable income from personal assets.)

Better for us never
To know a father. If only
You could never know your mother!

So be nice, be clever.
Adventurers, in setting forth
Have never a thought for your begetter.
But zoom on in that eternity
Promised by your patron, your donor,
By your ever-dying poet
Who remains
Your humble servant.

JAMES KIRKUP

A PRACTICAL WOMAN

"O who'll get me a healthy child:—
    I should prefer a son—
Seven have I had in thirteen years,
    Sickly every one!

"Three mope about as feeble shapes;
    Weak; white; they'll be no good.
One came deformed; an idiot next;
    And two are crass as wood.

"I purpose one not only sound
    In flesh, but bright in mind:
And duly for producing him
    A means I've now to find."

She went away. She disappeared,
    Years, years. Then back she came:
In her hand was a blooming boy
    Mentally and in frame.

"I found a father at last who'd suit
    The purpose in my head,
And used him till he'd done his job,"
    Was all thereon she said.

THOMAS HARDY

"SAID JIM X . . ."

        Said Jim X . . .:
There once was a pore honest sailor, a heavy drinker,
A hell of a cuss, a rowster, a boozer, and
The drink finally sent him to hospital,
And they operated, and there was a poor whore in
The woman's ward had a kid, while
They were fixing the sailor, and they brought him the kid
When he came to, and said:
        "Here! this is what we took out of you."

An' he looked at it, an' he got better,
And when he left the hospital, quit the drink,
And when he was well enough
        signed on with another ship
And saved up his pay money,
        and kept on savin' his pay money,
And bought a share in the ship,
        and finally had half shares,
Then a ship
        and in time a whole line of steamers;
And educated the kid,
        and when the kid was in college,

The ole sailor was again taken bad
          and the doctors said he was dying,
And the boy came to the bedside,
          and the old sailor said:
"Boy, I'm sorry I can't hang on a bit longer,
"You're young yet.
          I leave you re-sponsa-bilities.
"Wish I could ha' waited till you were older,
"More fit to take over the bisness . . ."
          "But, father,
"Don't, don't talk about me, I'm all right,
"It's you, father."
          "That's it, boy, you said it.
"You called me your father, and I ain't.
"I ain't your dad, no,
"I am not your fader but your moder," quod he,
"Your fader was a rich merchant in Stambouli."

EZRA POUND

From A Draft of XXX Cantos, XII

INFANT SONG

Don't you love my baby, mam,
Lying in his little pram,

Polished all with water clean,
The finest baby ever seen?

Daughter, daughter, if I could
I'd love your baby as I should,

But why the suit of signal red,
The horns that grow out of his head,

Why does he burn with brimstone heat,
Have cloven hooves instead of feet,

Fishing hooks upon each hand,
The keenest tail that's in the land,

Pointed ears and teeth so stark
And eyes that flicker in the dark?

Don't you love my baby, mam?

Dearest, I do not think I can.
I do not, do not think I can.

CHARLES CAUSLEY

SONG FOR THE INFANT JUDAS

There's raw meat for the tiger cub,
There's beech-mast for the swine,
In polar seas the plankton please
Cold codlings when they dine;
But, O, my Lord and Master,
Was this an act of grace,
Your child to bring to a field of spring
Then turn away your face?

The mystery of God's grace!

A baby comes here crying,
A chicken goes, "cheep, cheep",
Each in their way all creatures say
That life is where they weep,
But when the red man's mother
Had brought her child to bed
It barked aloud and in a crowd
The people turned and fled.

They fled, the people fled.

O, when we offered ribbons
To deck his first birthday
And sugar plums for tender gums
To take the grief away,
He did not smile or dimple
But gasped as if the air
Was sharp and thin that he breathed in
And more than he could bear.

Lord, how much can we bear?

THOMAS BLACKBURN

THE DEATH OF THE BALL
TURRET GUNNER

From my mother's sleep I fell into the State,
And I hunched in its belly till my wet fur froze.
Six miles from earth, loosed from its dream of life,
I woke to black flak and the nightmare fighters.
When I died they washed me out of the turret with a
    hose.

RANDALL JARRELL

"IN THE YEAR 1945 AN ORIGINAL
CHILD   WAS BORN"
Points for Meditation to be Scratched on the Walls of a Cave

1: In the year 1945 an Original Child was born. The name
Original Child was given to it by the Japanese people, who
recognized that it was the first of its kind.

2: On April 12th, 1945, Mr Harry Truman became the
President of the United States, which was then fighting the
second world war. Mr Truman was a vice president who
became president by accident when his predecessor died of a
cerebral hemorrhage. He did not know as much about the war
as the president before him did. He knew a lot less about the
war than many people did.

About one hour after Mr Truman became president, his aides
told him about a new bomb which was being developed by
atomic scientists. They called it the "atomic bomb". They said
scientists had been working on it for six years and that it had so

far cost two billion dollars. They added that its power was equal to that of twenty thousand tons of TNT. A single bomb could destroy a city. One of those present added, in a reverent tone, that the new explosive might eventually destroy the whole world.

But Admiral Leahy told the President the bomb would never work.

3: President Truman formed a committee of men to tell him if this bomb would work, and if so, what he should do with it . . .

4: In June 1945 the Japanese government was taking steps to negotiate for peace. The Japanese High Command was not in favor of asking for peace, but wanted to continue the war, even if the Japanese mainland were invaded. The generals believed that the war should continue until everybody was dead. The Japanese generals were professional soldiers.

5: In the same month of June, the President's committee decided that the new bomb should be dropped on a Japanese city. This would be a demonstration of the bomb on a civil and military target. As "demonstration" it would be a kind of a "show". "Civilians" all over the world love a good "show". The "destructive" aspect of the bomb would be "military".

*

7: There was discussion about which city should be selected as the first target. Some wanted it to be Kyoto, an ancient capital of Japan and a center of the Buddhist religion. Others said no, this would cause bitterness. As a result of a chance conversation, Mr Stimson, the Secretary of War, had recently read up on the history and beauties of Kyoto. He insisted that this city should be left untouched. Some wanted Tokyo to be the first target, but others argued that Tokyo had already been practically destroyed by fire raids and could no longer be considered a "target". So it was decided Hiroshima was the most opportune target, as it had not yet been bombed at all. Lucky Hiroshima! What others had experienced over a period of four years would happen to Hiroshima in a single day! Much time would be saved, and "time is money"!

8: When they bombed Hiroshima they would put the following out of business: the Ube Nitrogen Fertilizer Company; the Ube Soda Company; the Nippon Motor Oil Company; the Sumitoma Chemical Company; the Sumitoma Aluminum Company; and most of the inhabitants.

*

13: The time was coming for the new bomb to be tested, in the New Mexico desert. A name was chosen to designate this secret operation. It was called "Trinity".

14: At 5.30 a.m. on July 16th, 1945 a plutonium bomb was successfully exploded in the desert at Almagordo, New Mexico. It was suspended from a hundred foot steel tower which evaporated. There was a fireball a mile wide. The great flash could be seen for a radius of 250 miles. A blind woman miles away said she perceived light. There was a cloud of smoke 40,000 feet high. It was shaped like a toadstool.

15: Many who saw the experiment expressed their satisfaction in religious terms. A semi-official report even quoted a religious book—The New Testament, "Lord, I believe, help thou my unbelief." There was an atmosphere of devotion. It was a great act of faith. They believed the explosion was exceptionally powerful.

16: Admiral Leahy, still a "doubting Thomas", said that the bomb would not explode when dropped from a plane over a city. Others may have had "faith", but he had his ow... of "hope".

22: On August 1st the bomb was assembled in an airconditioned hut on Tinian. Those who handled the bomb referred to it as "Little Boy". Their care for the Original Child was devoted and tender.

*

25: On August 4th the bombing crew on Tinian watched a movie of "Trinity" (the Almagordo Test). August 5th was a Sunday but there was little time for formal worship. They said a quick prayer that the war might end "very soon". On that day, Col. Tibbetts, who was in command of the B-29 that was to drop the bomb, felt that his bomber ought to have a name. He baptized it Enola Gay, after his mother in Iowa. Col. Tibbetts was a well balanced man, and not sentimental. He did not have a nervous breakdown after the bombing, like some of the other members of the crew.

26: On Sunday afternoon "Little Boy" was brought out in procession and devoutly tucked away in the womb of Enola Gay. That evening few were able to sleep. They were as excited as little boys on Christmas Eve.

27: At 1.37 a.m. August 6th the weather scout plane took off. It was named the Straight Flush, in reference to the mechanical action of a water closet. There was a picture of one, to make this evident.

28: At the last minute before taking off Col. Tibbetts changed the secret radio call sign from "Visitor" to "Dimples". The Bombing Mission would be a kind of flying smile.

*

31: At 3.09 they reached Hiroshima and started the bomb run. The city was full of sun. The fliers could see the green grass in the gardens. No fighters rose up to meet them. There was no flak. No one in the city bothered to take cover.

32: The bomb exploded within 100 feet of the aiming point. The fireball was 18,000 feet across. The temperature at the center of the fireball was 100,000,000 degrees. The people who were near the center became nothing. The whole city was blown to bits and the ruins all caught fire instantly everywhere, burning briskly. 70,000 people were killed right away or died within a few hours. Those who did not die at once suffered great pain. Few of them were soldiers.

33: The men in the plane perceived that the raid had been successful, but they thought of the people in the city and they were not perfectly happy. Some felt they had done wrong. But in any case they had obeyed orders. "It was war."

*

35: It took a little while for the rest of Japan to find out what had happened to Hiroshima. Papers were forbidden to publish any news of the new bomb. A four line item said that Hiroshima had been hit by incendiary bombs and added: "It seems that some damage was caused to the city and its vicinity."

36: Then the military governor of the Prefecture of Hiroshima issued a proclamation full of martial spirit. To all the people without hands, without feet, with their faces falling off, with their intestines hanging out, with their whole bodies full of radiation, he declared: "We must not rest a single day in our war effort . . . We must bear in mind that the annihilation of the stubborn enemy is our road to revenge." He was a professional soldier.

*   *

38: On August 9th another bomb was dropped on Nagasaki, though Hiroshima was still burning. On August 11th the Emperor overruled his high command and accepted the peace terms dictated at Potsdam. Yet for three days discussion continued, until on August 14th the surrender was made public and final.

*

40: As to the Original Child that was now born, President Truman summed up the philosophy of the situation in a few words. "We found the bomb" he said "and we used it."

41: Since that summer many other bombs have been "found". What is going to happen? At the time of writing, after a season of brisk speculation, men seem to be fatigued by the whole question.

THOMAS MERTON
From "Original Child Bomb"

GLOSSARY

aiblins   perhaps
aiver   carthorse
asklent   askew

bienly   warmly
birkie   spry fellow
bob   bunch
bobbing   mocking
boost   ought
botargoes   a fish-roe dish
braw   fine
BVD   trademark, used for underwear
bulbul   songbird of the thrush family, 'nightingale' of the
   East

cheels   lads
clauted   drained
clish ma claver   blathering
clouted   patched
coggie   large drinking bowl
couthie   kind, loving
cowte   colt
craft   croft

dall   hand
daut   caress
dauted   spoiled
dint   occasion, severe blow
dousely   decorously

enuwyd freshened

fa' befall
fash trouble
frely foyde noble child
funny sportive

galah rose-breasted cockatoo
get offspring
Gul rose (Persian)

heting promise
hight called
hirples hobbles

kintra country
kukoo Afro-Barbadian dish with secret ancestral connotations

laggen the angle between the side and the bottom of a cask
lapped wrapped
lissed comforted
londe livelong

mailins acres, leased small-holding
mischanter mishap
mop baby

nepte catmint
NHS National Health Service

okro okra, West Indian plant whose pods are used for soup or as a vegetable
ouzles blackbirds

plack farthing

queir   choir

reflaring   giving off scent
reft   broken
reif   thieving, plunder
rulled   turned

Saint Geoffrey's Day   never, since there is no saint of the
   name
spairges   bespatters
spinks   finches, especially the chaffinch
stocked   leased
stounds   pangs
stoure   dust
string   a measure
susum   susumba, aromatic plant with berries used for
   preparing soups, fish, etc.

tack   tenure, leasehold
tarrowt   tarried, hesitated
Tiki   Maori creator god
Tilley   paraffin lamp
tint   lost

wared   cursed
warlo   warlock
Wasp   White Anglo-Saxon Protestant
wean   child
winna ding   won't be shifted

INDEX OF FIRST LINES

INDEX OF POETS AND WORKS

ACKNOWLEDGEMENTS

For permission to reprint copyright material the publishers gratefully acknowledge the following:

Hutchinson Publishing Group Ltd for 'Ode to Me' from *Collected Poems* by Kingsley Amis; W.W. Norton & Company, Inc. for 'Christmas Eve' from *Collected Poems 1951–1971* by A. R. Ammons, Copyright © 1972 by A. R. Ammons; Faber & Faber Ltd for 'Mundus et Infans', 'Many Happy Returns (for John Rettger)' from *Collected Poems* of W. H. Auden and for 'Birthday Poem (to Christopher Isherwood)' from *The English Auden* by W. H. Auden; Granada Publishing Ltd for 64 lines from 'Today, the twenty-sixth of February', no. 9, from *The True Confession of George Barker*, and Faber & Faber Ltd for 'For the Fourth Birthday of my Daughter' from *Poems of Places and People* by George Barker; Unicorn Press, PO Box 3307, Greensboro, NC 27402, for 'on the birth of dan goldman' from *Prison Poems* by Daniel Berrigan, Copyright © 1973 by Daniel Berrigan; Farrar, Straus and Giroux, Inc. and Faber & Faber Ltd for an excerpt from 'Homage to Mistress Bradstreet', Copyright © 1956 by John Berryman, and for 'Hello' and 'Your Birthday in Wisconsin You Are 140' from *Delusions*, Copyright © 1969, 1971 by John Berryman, Copyright © 1972 by the Estate of John Berryman; John Murray (Publishers) Ltd and John Betjeman for 'For Patrick: aetat LXX' from *Collected Poems* and for 'For the Queen Mother' by John Betjeman; the Canadian Publishers, McClelland and Stewart Ltd of Toronto, for 'Birthday' from *Fall by Fury* by Earle Birney; Anthony Sheil Associates Ltd and MacGibbon and Kee for 'Song for the Infant Judas' from *The Fourth Man* by Thomas Blackburn; Oxford University Press for 'Cherries', Parts 1, 3 and 4, from *Mother Poem* by Edward Kamau Brathwaite, Copyright © 1977 by Edward Kamau Brathwaite; Harper & Row Publishers, Inc. for 'The birth in a narrow room', Copyright 1949 by Gwendolyn Brooks Blakely and for 'Jessie Mitchell's Mother', Copyright © 1960 by Gwendolyn Brooks, both from *The World of Gwendolyn Brooks*; David Higham Associates Ltd and Macmillan Publishers for 'Infant Song' and 'The Animals' Carol' from *Collected Poems* by Charles Causley; Miss D. E. Collins and J. M. Dent & Sons Ltd for 'By the Babe Unborn' from *The Collected Poems* of G. K. Chesterton; John Ciardi and Rutgers University Press for 'The Evil Eye' from *Lives of X* by John Ciardi, © 1951 by Rutgers, the State University, and W. W. Norton & Company, Inc. for 'Birthday' from *For Instance*, Copyright © 1979 by John Ciardi; J. M. Dent & Sons Ltd for 'To an Infant Daughter' and 'The Mother's Lullaby' from *The Poems of John Clare* edited by J. W. and A. Tibble; Jack Clemo for

Publishers, Sydney, for 'A Letter to David Campbell on the Birthday of W. B. Yeats, 1965' from *A Late Picking: Poems 1965–1974* by A. D. Hope; the Society of Authors as the literary representatives of the Estate of A. E. Housman and Jonathan Cape Ltd, publishers of A. E. Housman's *Collected Poems*, for 'Loveliest of trees, the cherry now'; Alfred A. Knopf, Inc. for 'Birth' from *Fields of Wonder* by Langston Hughes, Copyright © 1947 by Langston Hughes; Faber & Faber Ltd for 'Ravens' and 'Birth of Rainbow' from *Moortown* by Ted Hughes, 'Salmon Eggs' from *Selected Poems 1957–1981* by Ted Hughes and 'Examination at the Womb-Door' from *Crow* by Ted Hughes; Faber & Faber Ltd and Harper & Row Publishers, Inc. for 'Childbirth' from *The Hawk in the Rain* by Ted Hughes, Copyright © 1957 by Ted Hughes; Faber & Faber Ltd and Farrar, Straus & Giroux, Inc. for 'The Death of the Ball Turret Gunner' from *Randall Jarrell, The Complete Poems*, Copyright 1945, 1969 by Mrs Randall Jarrell, renewed © 1973 by Mrs Randall Jarrell; David Higham Associates Ltd and Macmillan Publishers Ltd for 'A Birthday in Hospital' from *Collected Poems* by Elizabeth Jennings; Carcanet New Press Ltd for 'To My Mother at 73' from *Consequently I Rejoice* and 'Meditation on the Nativity' from *Growing Points* by Elizabeth Jennings; Katherine B. Kavanagh for 'Ante Natal Dream' and 'Candida' from *Collected Poems of Patrick Kavanagh*; Chatto & Windus Ltd for 'Birthday' from *Selected Poems* by P. J. Kavanagh (originally published in *On the Way to the Depot*); Curtis Brown Ltd, New York, for 'Birth Report' from *Growing into Love*, Copyright © 1969 by X. J. Kennedy; the National Trust for 'A Nativity' by Rudyard Kipling from *Rudyard Kipling's Verse*; James Kirkup for 'To My Children Unknown, Produced by Artificial Insemination' from *White Shadows Black Shadows* by James Kirkup, published by J. M. Dent & Sons Ltd; the Marvell Press for 'Born Yesterday' from *The Less Deceived* by Philip Larkin; Chatto & Windus Ltd for 'Years Later' from *Directions of Memory* by Laurence Lerner; The Executors of the Estate of C. Day Lewis, the Hogarth Press and Jonathan Cape Ltd for 'Though bodies are apart' from *From Feathers to Iron* from *Collected Poems* (1954) by C. Day Lewis; Press Porcépic for 'Serenade for Strings' from *The Woman I Am* by Dorothy Livesay; Faber & Faber Ltd and Farrar, Straus & Giroux, Inc. for 'Marriage: "11. Ninth Month", "13. Robert Sheridan Lowell", "14. Overhanging Cloud"' from *The Dolphin* by Robert Lowell, Copyright © 1973 Robert Lowell; the Hogarth Press Ltd for 'The Seven Houses. In Memory of John F. Kennedy' from *Poems New and Selected* by George Mackay Brown; the Hogarth Press Ltd for 'Unposted Birthday Card' from *Tree of Strings* by Norman MacCaig; Faber & Faber Ltd for 'Cradle Song for Miriam', 'Prayer Before Birth' and 'Day of Renewal' from *The Collected Poems of Louis MacNeice*; Granada Publishing Ltd for 'Arteries juicy with blood' from 'Lines Concerning the Unknown Soldier' from *Poems* by Osip Mandelstam, translated by James Greene; Maori poem 'Give Me My Infant Now' from *The Penguin Book of Oral Poetry*, original source *The Ancient History of the Maori* by John White (G. Didsbury, Wellington, 1887–1890); Mrs Ellen C. Masters for an excerpt from 'Tomorrow is my Birthday' from *Selected Poems* by Edgar Lee